Hallowed Hills, Holy Waters

In the Great Smoky Mountains

By Greg Hoover

Hallowed Hills, Holy Waters:
In the Great Smoky Mountains

Copyright © 2014 Greg Hoover

Printed by CreateSpace.com in the USA

ISBN-13: 978-1496191793

ISBN-10: 149619179X

Photo Credits

Front Cover:
- Andrews Bald by Phyllis Hoover

Back Cover
- Waterfall on Porters Creek by Keith Oakes
- Fontana Lake by Melissa Ballinger

Climb the mountains and get their good tidings. Nature's peace will flow into you as sunshine flows into trees. The winds will blow their own freshness into you, and the storms their energy, while cares will drop off like autumn leaves.

John Muir

Going to the mountains is like going home.

John Muir

Contents

Preface   1

Introduction   2

Chapter 1: Forney Creek   6

Chapter 2: Sixty-Eight Miles   22

Chapter 3: Ridges and Rivers   46

Chapter 4: Hazel Creek   62

Chapter 5: Long Rod, Short Cast   81

Chapter 6: Sunrise, Sunset, And Then Some   98

Chapter 7: Out Under the Moon of the Great Smokies   116

Chapter 8: Happy New Year   129

Chapter 9: Tsali's Revenge   140

Chapter 10: A Day in the Middle of Everything   163

Chapter 11: Doxology   176

Epilogue: Do It Yourself   180

Preface

I wasn't born in the Smoky Mountains, but I got here as quick as I could. I love the Smokies, and I'm privileged to live just an hour away from them, but maybe it's just as well that I didn't grow up here because I might have yielded to that human tendency of taking one's home for granted. In fact, I did yield. I grew up in that flat, humid region of America known as central Florida, and I'll freely admit that I now totally and willingly take that land of my childhood for granted. It was easy. My first love, since the age of five, has been the mountains, particularly the Great Smoky Mountains.

There are reasons why we call the Smoky Mountains "great," and this book is about these mountains and those reasons. It's a book of stories about canoeing across a lake and into the mountain wilderness, hiking for a week along the crest of the Smokies, walking next to rivers and in rivers, watching the sun set and darkness fall in complete solitude, hiking by moonlight, and seducing mountain trout. It's about a land the Cherokee called *shaconage* – the land of blue smoke.

So, consider these paragraphs your invitation to explore these Great Smoky Mountains, especially the off-the-main-road peaks and valleys that will get you away from the crowds and into the heart of the wilderness. In the process, you'll discover how to immerse yourself in some of the Smokies' special places, such as Mount Le Conte and Mount Cammerer; Hazel Creek and Forney Creek; High Rocks and Andrews Bald; the Little River and the Little Pigeon River.

As you read about the people, places, and history of the Great Smoky Mountains National Park, you'll better understand why we call these mountains *Great*.

Introduction

Several years ago I spent some time reading hundred year old volumes of the Sierra Club's magazine. The Sierra Club was founded by John Muir and a few other kindred spirits in 1892 to promote the protection of the Yosemite Valley and America's other natural wonders. Muir was an unconventional, philosophical, and passionate writer/hiker who once spent a few hours in the top of a Douglas Fir during a windstorm to better understand how the tree experienced the storm. Or, as he put it, "to obtain a wider outlook and get my ear close to the Aeolian music of its topmost needles." The guy was eccentric and eloquent, a potent combination which makes for good stories.

In one of Muir's articles from the early 1900s he described a magnificent national monument in Arizona that had recently been set aside by President Theodore Roosevelt. Yes, there was a time when Americans had to be told about the Grand Canyon which would soon become one of our most popular and cherished national parks. Unlike many of us who are reluctant to advertise our secret, special places, Muir was happy to spill the beans.

One of his most mind-bending articles was about Yellowstone National Park. After eloquently and passionately describing its glories, he went on to suggest that more roads be built in the park. *More* roads? If you know anything about the Sierra Club, then your mind is probably bending just as mine did when I first read it. "More roads" just doesn't fit the Sierra Club agenda which, simply put, is: development bad, wilderness good. It would be like Teddy Roosevelt, a friend of Muir's, writing about the joys of pacifism. What was Muir thinking?

Well, first of all, this was over 100 years ago, there weren't many roads in Yellowstone, and maybe a few more wouldn't have hurt anything. But more importantly, Muir knew that in order to protect the national parks, they needed a group of people who had seen their beauty, had fallen in love with them, and would fight to protect them, because we protect what we love. Remember, the idea of national parks was still fairly new and a bit controversial, so access was a necessary part of the process.

This was an odd twist in America's growing love affair with the outdoors in which expanding cities, increasing prosperity, and technological change (mainly in the form of automobiles and asphalt) were combining to create something new in American history – middle class tourists with the time, money, and means to travel. While cities, money, cars, and pavement are usually seen as a threat to the wild outdoors, they were actually creating the constituency that would save the great outdoors for future generations. National parks were quickly becoming America's playground.

It's ironic, then, that today our national parks are being overrun by those who love them. I don't know whether it's a Tragedy of the Commons or a Self-Fulfilling Prophecy, or both. You go to visit your favorite park, thus adding to the crowds and pollution that make it stressful to visit. You become part of the crowd that you wish would just go away, knowing that the crowds are there for the same reasons you are. It's a feeling every trout fisherman has about his favorite river and every hiker her favorite trail. Or, as Yogi Berra allegedly said about a restaurant in New York City, "Nobody goes there any more... it's too crowded."

Most of our national parks face this dilemma, including the Great Smoky Mountains, so anyone who visits the Smokies has to deal with the crowds. Indeed, every summer and fall several million Smokies visitors "deal with the crowds" by diving in and becoming part of the teeming masses, yearning to breathe free, creating traffic jams of Biblical proportions in which the best survival strategy is to have a full tank of gas, a working air conditioner, and distractions for the kids. It also helps to have visited a bathroom recently because there's not much privacy in four lanes of an asphalt swamp. It's all high adventure for anyone who enjoys watching grass grow, paint dry, or cars idle, which apparently some people do.

Fortunately, there are less stressful ways of dealing with the crowds. Some local folks simply choose to hibernate during the summer, venturing into the park only in the off-season months of November through March. They spend the warm months playing golf and doing yard work, which do have the advantage of being outdoor activities... not unlike working on a chain gang. I just can't bring myself to surrender the park to the crowds for half the year because I can hear the ticking of my biological clock, and it gets a little louder and a little slower with each passing year, so I've begun pruning my life's To Do list to the bare essentials. I mean, maybe you *can* teach a pig to sing, but unless you really, really need a singing pig, there are probably better ways to spend your time. So learning to play the piano, mastering Spanish, and teaching a pig to sing have become lost causes for me because time is running short, while spending more time on the ridges and in the rivers of the Smokies has jumped to near the top of my list.

And so, my strategy for dealing with the crowds is to avoid them by exploring the far-flung nooks and crannies of the park, twelve months out of the year; which, of course, means getting off the main roads.

But aren't all the best attractions on the main roads? First of all, let's not call them attractions, okay? If you want attractions, go south about 700 miles. There's a place down there... maybe you've heard of it... it's called Disney World. Second, yes the most popular spots are on the main roads, but *popular* is not necessarily *best*. In fact, all *popular* really means is *crowded*. It comes from the Latin word *populus* meaning "people." Or, to paraphrase a bit, lots of people. Crowds.

Most of these spots are popular – I mean, crowded – not because they are more fabulous and breath-taking than the rest of the park but simply because they are so easy to get to. Let's take Newfound Gap right in the middle of the park as an example. This is the point at which the road from Gatlinburg to Cherokee reaches the main crest. Sure it has a fine view, but it's definitely not the best view in the Smokies. Yet it is hugely popular. Why? Because it's the main parking lot on the main road. If the road crossed the main crest a couple of miles to the east or the west, then *that* spot would be the hugely popular spot. In fact, in the old pioneer days, the main route across the Smokies did cross at a different spot, but explorers *found a new gap* in the 1850s, and when preparations were being made to improve and pave the road in the 1920s, the surveyors re-routed the road through this "new found" gap. Thus the name.

Or, the Loop – the spot on the main road where the switchbacks are so tight that at one point the road just circles around and crosses over itself. I've seen postcards of it, as if it were some great natural wonder. If you've never seen it in person, get ready for a disappointment. It's just not that big a deal. It's a moderately neat bit of road construction in a pretty place. But that's all it is. It's only slightly more dramatic than getting off the interstate and then driving back around on the overpass. I suppose a civil engineer might see some majesty in it, the way my mechanic can get misty-eyed about a well-made transmission. So if you are an engineer, don't miss it. (I'll admit that the stonework on the bridges in the park is so well done that it could almost qualify as art, but skillful stonework isn't why we go to the Smokies. After all, there's no book for sale in the visitor centers entitled *Bridges of the Smokies*. It would be mind-numbingly repetitive, I would think.)

I guess what I'm saying is that the main roads through the park have plenty of nice spots on them – picnic areas, scenic views, noisy rivers, quiet walkways, Newfound Gap, Clingmans Dome, Cades Cove – but these are not, by any stretch of the imagination, the only highlights of the park. You can see a lot of great stuff away from the crowded, main roads, but it might take a little extra effort on your part.

Take Forney Creek for example…

Chapter 1
Forney Creek

Forney Creek is the kind of place that's easy to overlook. It's only a three mile walk or a three mile paddle to get to it, so it's accessible but only to those who are committed to going there. You're not likely to stumble upon it on your way to someplace else because it's not really on the way to anywhere else. Like just about every square inch of the Smokies, Forney Creek is pretty, so it's worth visiting, but it doesn't have anything to make it stand out from the crowd. It's not the highest or oldest or prettiest or most isolated or *most* anything. It's great, but without renown, like the offensive line of a football team with a Heisman running back, which is exactly what we're looking for – beauty without the paparazzi.

I've never actually walked to Forney; although, I've paddled a kayak there a few times. The thing that makes it difficult to paddle to is not the water or the distance. It's finding the road to the boat ramp and then making the long, winding drive to it. It's the kind of place that you have to know someone who knows about it. Even then, they might not be able to tell you how to get there. I honestly don't remember and can't imagine how I managed to find it for the first time – probably some combination of maps, trial & error, and divine intervention.

If you go to Bryson City, you can ask someone there about it. I don't know the name of the boat ramp, but I suspect that most people who use this put-in don't know the official name of it either. Just ask for the boat ramp across from Forney Creek, but don't be surprised if they tell you that "you cain't get there from here." There are lots of places like that in the Southern Appalachians, and this is one of them.

The easy directions are that you take State Road 1313 until it ends at the boat ramp. Simple enough, if you can find SR

1313. To find it, just take SR 1312 until 1313 splits off of it. To get to 1312, just take 1311 until 1312 splits off of it. All these have green street signs with the SR number on them. All of them except, for some unknown reason, SR 1311, the first road you need to find. You can get to 1311 by taking Old US 19 which splits off of US 19 at the edge of town. Of course, there are a couple of places to get on Old US 19.... Like they say in Bryson City, you can't get there from here. So, good luck with that.

Walking to Forney is perhaps a little easier. In fact, it was almost incredibly easy. We all came within a whisker of being able to *drive* to Forney and beyond. To see the evidence, just go to Bryson City and find Lakeview Drive – also known as the Road to Nowhere – and drive to its end, which is abrupt. I'm pleased that the Road to Nowhere goes by that name rather than the Road to Forney Creek or the Road to Hazel Creek. In fact, I suppose my favorite kind of road is the kind that goes to Nowhere, preferably the Middle of Nowhere.

So why is Lakeview Drive the Road to Nowhere rather than the Road to Somewhere? The original boundaries of the park when it was established in 1934 were very similar to what they are today. The main exception was in this southwest quadrant of the park. The original boundary was a few miles north of its present location. The Little Tennessee River, Forney Creek, Hazel Creek and Eagle Creek were, for the most part, not in the park. In 1943 Fontana Dam was built, flooding the Little Tennessee River from Fontana Dam east to Bryson City. It also flooded the road that ran along the banks of the Little Tennessee, connecting Bryson City with points west. When the Federal government annexed the north shore of the new Fontana Lake, thus expanding the park's boundary to the center line of Fontana Lake, it promised to build a new road through this annexed portion to replace the road that now lay at the bottom of the lake. This new road would not only provide access to Fontana and beyond, it would also provide access to the numerous family cemeteries scattered along the creeks flowing out of the park and into Fontana Lake. These are the small cemeteries that you'll bump into whenever you hike along a major waterway in the Smokies.

The road construction began in the 1960s and extended about five miles into the park from Bryson City, across Noland Creek, but it stopped about two miles short of Forney Creek. Construction was halted due to budget problems and environmental concerns; various studies were done and proposals were made in the subsequent years, and the project was finally, completely abandoned in 2010. The Lakeview Drive would forever go to Nowhere In Particular. Forney Creek would remain a three mile walk from the end of the road.

My daughter, her husband, and I wound along the twisting two-lane to the shores of Fontana Lake. We had my kayak and canoe in tow as we passed a variety of cabins, houses, and trailers in varying stages of disrepair. This is by no means a resort community; although, as you get closer to the lake, you'll get an occasional glimpse of an expensive gate across a nicely paved driveway. But this is still one of those poor-to-working-class, rural areas that has a lot of simple, local character. Almost every home has a pickup truck in the yard, and it would not be a bit out of place to see a dead bear hanging from a tree branch and a pen of Plott hounds out behind the house. It also seems like the kind of place that might have a few moonshine stills and modest marijuana gardens. Although, let's make it clear that I've never seen either of those. Let's make it even more clear that I've never even looked and don't intend to. (A certain breed of rural folks can make it known in no uncertain terms that a guy ought to mind his own business, which is a code of conduct I intend to honor, especially on SR 1312.) I'm pretty sure they all have indoor plumbing; although, an occasional outhouse wouldn't be a complete surprise either.

We easily stored two night's worth of camping gear in our canoe and kayak and paddled about a mile west down the main channel and about two miles up the Forney Creek channel. When the water finally ended, we were at the moveable mouth of Forney Creek. It was mid-October, so the water was low because TVA generates power all summer and fall by running water out of the lake through the bottom of the dam. When lake levels drop in the fall, the mouths of the rivers flowing out of the park and into the lake are covered with a lot of soft, muddy, bare land that would be underwater during the spring and summer. When the water levels are high from the spring rains, the mouth of the river will move fifty yards or more upstream to the edge of the forest.

So the most pleasant time to visit is the early summer because you can paddle right to the edge of the forest. As soon as you step out of your boat you are surrounded by trees, shrubs, and flowers. By October the water level has dropped and you step out into a moist, lunar landscape. It's just one more reminder that this lake, as beautiful as it is, is human-made and human-controlled. If scenic beauty were the main point, TVA would keep it full, but the phrase "scenic beauty" probably doesn't show up in TVA's mission statement. It's all about power – electrical power, that is. The beauty of the lake is merely a pleasant by-product.

This human factor used to annoy me until I realized an inescapable fact: most of life's necessities and conveniences have been manipulated by humans. Homes, clothes, and roads come most immediately to mind, but even our food and pets are joint efforts between nature and people. Corn began as a grass that we selectively-pollinated, resulting in the large ears of corn we have today. Or, your dog started out as a wolf or jackal that was genetically molded by people who wanted a domesticated canine for some specific purpose, such as herding sheep or chasing badgers. That's why there are no packs of wild poodles roaming the mountains and no "Do Not Feed The Dachshunds" signs in the backcountry. Like corn, those creatures don't exist in the wild. They were created by humans for humans. Human ingenuity is often beneficial, sometimes amazing, and on rare occasions beautiful, as in the case of art, poetry, and Fontana Lake.

Even though this was prime leaf season, we saw only three trucks and trailers at the boat ramp and just one boat on the lake this afternoon. All the leaf watchers were clogging Cades Cove and Newfound Gap Road, as well as the roads in Pigeon Forge, Gatlinburg, Townsend, and Cherokee. The sky was a crisp, robin egg blue, so at least all those folks stuck in traffic had a nice day to do it in. In my more generous moments, I feel a tinge of sympathy for them because at least they tried to get outdoors and enjoy something without wires, silicon chips, and electricity, but that sympathy is quickly overshadowed by the sense of superiority that arises in the heart of anyone who has inside information about the secret workings of life, the best way to see the colors of a Smoky Mountain autumn being just one salient example.

The Lower Forney Creek campsite was less than a quarter mile from the mouth of the creek, so we brought a little more equipment than we normally would – a couple of folding camp chairs were the main additions to our sparse backpacking paraphernalia. Setting up camp was familiar and pleasant. My small tent smelled of dirt, leaves, and smoke, which is exactly how a tent should smell. Whenever I set up my tent, I think of where the dirt in it came from, and I spend a moment reliving that previous trip. This time it was Hazel Creek in May. It was the fishing trip that got blown out by a full day of rain. As I recall, I caught one small brook trout on a Parachute Adams, probably a size 16, in Sugar Fork before the water got too muddy and high. Instead of fishing for two days, we fished for 30 minutes then lay in our tents or sat under trees with our rain jackets cinched tight, eating granola bars and jerky. To add insult to injury, after the trip I set up my tent in the yard to dry, and a neighborhood dog who is normally one of my best playmates came by and peed on it. When I saw him raise his leg, I paused for a second then actually laughed out loud. He and I both seemed to know it was somehow appropriate – a wet ending to a wet trip. A yellow exclamation point to emphasize the magnitude of the disaster. Dogs tend to have a middle school sense of humor, which means they sometimes get carried away and there's a mess to clean up afterward.

As evening approached, Melissa and John sat in their camp chairs by the small fire they had built. Wood is not plentiful at these backcountry sites, but we can always find enough downed wood if we'll just search away from the trail. I'm not much of a fire builder, which gives the appearance of a thoughtful, low impact, wilderness ethic, but the truth is simpler – I'm lazy. I like a campfire, but I can do without it. Fortunately, just about every other person on the planet enjoys a good camp fire, so unless I'm camping alone, I usually have a fire provided for me.

I felt guilty for letting Melissa and John do all the work, but not guilty enough to actually get up and help. In their youthful enthusiasm, I don't think they even noticed.

Normally, I'm ready to crawl in the tent and sleeping bag soon after darkness settles in, maybe reading for a while, but tonight will be different. The moon is high and bright, and the sky is clear, so I'm going to take advantage of it by walking back out to my kayak and paddling around the lake for an hour or two. This will be the first time I've done a night paddle, so I'm a bit apprehensive, even though there's no rational reason why it should be risky. Nevertheless, darkness adds a sense of uncertainty to just about any activity, even more when that activity is paddling a kayak on a cold, deep lake, alone.

As I walked out of the woods and into the muddy expanse, the silver glow of the moon gave the landscape a lunar look – silver, bare, alien. But the moon was so bright that it gave me an unexpected sense of security. My apprehension disappeared as soon as I stepped out of the forest and into the moon light and realized that visibility would not be a problem. My shadow stretched sharply to my right as I searched for solid spots in the soft, black dirt.

After about 10 minutes I reached the kayak and canoe that we had wedged between some exposed rocks a few feet above the shoreline. As I picked up my kayak, it banged against the rocks, scaring an animal in the woods about 100 feet away. It sounded loud enough to have been a bear, but I've been fooled before by the sound of a squirrel bounding through dry leaves. I'd guess that if the sound of thrashing leaves lasts only a second, then it's a squirrel who quickly found safe haven in a tree. If the thrashing goes on and on, it's probably a bear or deer or boar running for its life. It's almost always a squirrel, which is a little disappointing.

I perched like a clumsy heron on a small, shore-side rock and set the kayak in the water, parallel to the shore, never perpendicular with one end on land and the other in the water. That's a lesson that's quickly learned by every novice paddler, hopefully at a time and place with no witnesses. This is the evening's most tenuous moment as I'm trying to stay on this small rock to avoid the knee deep mud at the water's edge.

Stepping into the kayak, it wobbled a little, but it's a very stable craft so there were no Wile E. Coyote moments.

I pushed out into the still water and noticed for the first time that a slight breeze has been blowing from the north. I didn't even have to paddle. I let the breeze push me slowly, almost imperceptibly, down Forney Creek's flooded channel and toward the main channel of Fontana.

The main sound of the night was the rush of the creek flowing into the lake behind me. There were also the usual sounds of various insects and tree frogs. We'd had a few cold nights so far, but not enough to shut down their chorus for the season. There was also the sound of the breeze in the trees, rattling the drying leaves, but it was still too early in the season for there to be a heavy shower of leaves falling to the ground.

In the distance I hear an owl. It's a Great Horned Owl asking, "Who, who's awake? Me too." It's the classic owl hoot, and I consider hooting back, but before I can begin I hear another Great Horned answer from the other side of the channel. I listen to them ask and answer for several minutes. I'd like to think that they are reassuring each other that they are not alone in this big, cold world: "Be of good cheer; there are other kindred spirits haunting the dark woods." But I doubt that owls are that poetic, and knowing what I know about animals (including humans), it's more likely that they are taunting each other, establishing the boundaries of their territory – like gang graffiti sprayed on walls in rough, urban neighborhoods or bellicose politicians threatening one another. Fortunately, no fights break out tonight. Peace reigns on the lake. Although behind the scenes in the depths of the forest, mice and moles are dying at the hands of owls and bobcats. We live in a fallen world where death and domination are the rule, not the exception. It's a jungle out there, but the water ahead of me is dark and still.

On the water tonight, things are calm. I feel the breeze on the back of my neck. It's strong enough to push me along, but not strong enough to blow my hat off my head. The scene gets quieter as I glide 50, then 100 yards away from the mouth of the creek. The sounds of moving water are disappearing in the distance and the quiet of the still water is taking over.

The channel is about 50 yards across, and there are small ridges on both sides of me – I'm in a river valley, after all – so there's not a sense of vast expansiveness. That's a feeling that you get only on high mountain perches with those panoramic views. However, tonight my personal space is huge, having expanded from the few square feet of civilized life to a few square miles, thanks to being on a mountain lake at night.

The feeling in these flooded creek channels is one of length, height, and depth, but not breadth. I am actually sitting where the treetops should be. I imagine the rocks and logs and fallen timbers below me. Hunkered down in my kayak seat on the surface of the lake, I am actually up high, and my view is that of someone who has climbed to the top of a tree in a river valley to survey the landscape. Somewhere behind me stands Silers Bald; in front of me lays glowing, silver water and the trees and ridges of Nantahala National Forest.

Of course, the night sky provides a sense of expansiveness above. The moon is bold and dominant, enhancing the wildness of the scene, but at the same time it gives me a sense of security, like a little boy with a night light in his room. Sure, it helps you to see in the dark, but it also provides a sense of safety far beyond its tiny glow. It keeps the monsters in the closet where they belong.

Drifting on the lake at night is like a dream. The breeze creates a slight ripple on the surface of the water, and the glow of the moon on the ripples gives the effect of thousands of tiny flashbulbs – an array of random flashes, not quite simultaneous, a glistening that lasts and lasts and lasts as long as the breeze blows and the moon shines. Staring at it creates a psychedelic effect, so I stare for a while and time stands still.

Over the years since this Forney Creek trip, I've experimented with moonlit and moonless nights on Fontana, and I've come to prefer a bright moon. The reason is not entirely for the security of the night light. When I go out on the lake without a moon, I am hoping to experience a starry, starry night on the lake. I want to see the constellations and maybe a few meteors. I want to be overwhelmed by the Milky Way and the Big Dipper and all the other night time objects.

But moonless nights on the lake aren't quite as overwhelming as you'd expect. Sure, they are impressive, but the view of the stars is actually better once you get back on land and away from the lake because the lake surface is like a mirror; yes, a dim mirror, but definitely a mirror. It creates a glow, not a bright distracting glow like city lights; more of a background ambiance that gets in the way. The stars can't quite blaze and dazzle because of the interference from the glow of the lake. It's like trying to watch a movie while some guy in the audience is whispering to his buddies in a low pitched drone. You can't tell where it's coming from because it seems to be everywhere.

So, to get the full effect of the stars, stay on dry land. To get the full effect of the brightness of the moon, go to the lake. My paddle tonight is under a large, waxing moon, so when I stepped into my kayak an hour after sunset, the moon was already high in the sky, and both the sky and the water were glowing brightly.

After about an hour of drifting, I decided it was time to go back. So, I turned around and began paddling into the wind. The night sounds changed from insects, frogs, and owls to the hum of wind in my ear. All I could now hear was the blowing of the breeze, the "kurrl" of my paddles dipping alternately into the water, and the "plink, plink" of the ripples against the hull of the kayak. I pulled my hat down tighter on my head so it wouldn't blow off. My favorite headlamp is clipped to it, and I'd hate to lose them both in the water. If my hat blew off, I could probably paddle back and pick it up as it lingered on the surface, but it's an experiment that I'd rather not try, especially at night. You never know about those underwater monsters. They might be nocturnal… and hungry.

As I paddled back over 60+ years of mud and sediment that have been eroded away by Forney Creek, I began to hear the sound of the moving water again. I think about the many, many years that this erosion from mountains to seas has been going on and how our civilization has changed this process. Fontana Dam has created a lake where none previously existed. How many years will it take for the muddy entrances to all these feeder rivers to expand to fill in these channels? This mud should be in the Gulf of Mexico by now, but instead it's under and around me.

But I can't be too critical of modern civilization. In small doses, it can be comfortable, even beneficial. It's modern civilization that has given me not only this lake, but a plastic kayak to explore it with. It's given me the roads and the truck to turn a week-long trip from Jefferson City to Bryson City into a two hour drive. It's the glitz and glitter of modern life that attracts people to malls, movies, and TVs, keeping them off Fontana Lake so I can be alone tonight. Civilization has created many of the environmental problems that we face today, but it has also given us the equipment and opportunities to enjoy those parts of our world that we haven't yet despoiled. In fact, it's even given us the ability to get beyond the day to day battle to feed ourselves and to elevate our thoughts to pursue things like education, health, art, and love of the outdoors – the very outdoors that we almost eradicated. I hate irony. How ironic that life should have so much of it.

After my night paddle, I walked back across the mud flats and toward the opening in the woods where the trail to the campsite begins. When the lake is full in June and July, that opening would be at the water's edge, and this mudflat would be under water. Tonight I have to walk about a hundred yards to get there. Stepping out of the moonlight and onto the trail in the trees is like stepping into a dark tunnel. I turn on the headlamp on the brim of my hat and walk about five minutes back to the campsite. The only sounds I hear are the crunching of leaves under my feet and the relentless roar of the river a few yards away. They are the same sounds that a mountaineer would have heard 100 years ago, or the Cherokee 300 years ago. I feel the weight of nature and history surround me.

When I arrived back at the campsite, Melissa and John were still awake. Melissa was worried about me and had about decided to walk to the beached canoe to look for me. She and my wife often worry about me on my outdoor excursions. I think they worry too much, but maybe they have good reason because I have an affliction common to middle aged men: denial. A younger friend of mine has a pre-game mantra that his wife imposed upon him. He must repeat it before every recreation league basketball game: "I'm not 21 anymore. I'm not 21 anymore...." I probably need a similar ritual for the mountains, but it would be more discouraging than helpful: "I'm not 40 anymore. I'm not 40 anymore ...." Shoot, let's be honest: I'm not even 50 anymore.

When I was younger they worried that I'd do something stupid because I was young and thought I'd live forever. Now they worry that I'll get hurt while simply walking on a trail or climbing onto a river rock. When I do get seriously injured, it won't be from doing something incredibly stupid; it will happen by doing something that is safe and sensible for a guy in his 20s or 30s, but not for a guy in his 50s. When I end up with some broken bones or dehydrated from exposure, and someone asks me what happened, the short answer will be: "Not acting my age."

Later in the night, well after we had settled into our tents and sleeping bags, it started to rain. Rain on a tent fly, one of life's best sounds. We all slept well. Mud in the morning is a small price to pay for rain at night.

The next morning was cloudy and wet, but not rainy. I ate a brown and orange breakfast – cheese crackers, granola bars, ginger snap cookies, and filtered river water. Lunch will be the same, plus some peanut M&M's. One of the best things about hiking is that I can eat chocolate and peanuts with reckless abandon – a guiltless pleasure with no adverse consequences; although, I have discovered that if I hike more than 12 hours, something amazing and unexpected happens – I get tired of the chocolate and peanuts. That's something that has never happened in the other, civilized part of my life. It's one of those indescribable mysteries that can happen in the mountains.

After breakfast I took off on one more excursion – a seven mile hike up Bear Creek Trail to Welch Ridge and High Rocks. Melissa and John had decided to lounge around the campsite and attend to three essential campsite chores: eating, reading, and napping. Through self-discipline and sheer determination they managed to accomplish all three – several times – in the seven hours I was gone.

I didn't necessarily expect High Rocks to be the most dramatic spot in the mountains. In fact, I don't think there is a "most dramatic spot." There are numerous dramatic spots, and I don't waste my time debating which one is the very best. However, it did seem that High Rocks could be one of the most isolated spots in the park – a site rarely visited even by avid hikers. It's not a famous or dominant peak; although it is high, almost 5,200'. It is too far from any roads for it to be the destination of a reasonable day hike, the shortest route being a 10 mile (one way) walk from the Road to Nowhere. Twenty miles is the upper limit for a day hike for most folks.

High Rocks is not really "on the way" to anything famous. It's sort of on the way to Hazel Creek; although, it's near just one of several trails to Hazel. Actually, High Rocks is at the end of a half-mile, dead-end, side trail off Welch Ridge Trail, so to go there you have to intend to go there.

I'm sure some folks hike or ride their horses to High Rocks, but doing so just about requires an overnight stay at a backcountry campsite at Forney Creek or some other location. So, we've now eliminated about 99% of the park's visitors. I've only been there once, and it was on a weekday in mid October, so I don't have a lot of experience to draw from. All I can say is, I didn't see anyone else at High Rocks or on the trails.

So I set off on this cloudy, cool, almost-drizzly morning. I soon arrived at Bear Creek Trail and began ascending the eastern slope of Welch Ridge with Bear Creek flowing next to the trail. Like many trails in the Smokies this one is wide and smooth because it was once a railroad bed for the lumber companies of the early 1900s. The fall colors are vivid – mostly yellows at these lower elevations, with brilliant reds and corals kicking in at the higher elevations. I love *all* the colors, even brown, but there's something about the reds and corals that just makes me stop and stare, as if God had just invented them and was showing them to me to see what I thought about the idea.

There were enough dead leaves on the ground to make this hike noisy – a steady crunching of leaves with every step instead of the thumping and bumping of a summer hike. I'll drink heavily for these first 3 or 4 miles, then I'll stop at the Poplar

Flats campsite to refill before leaving the creek and ascending almost 2,000' in three miles to Welch Ridge.

The Poplar Flats campsite is a small, clean spot with room for about two tents. It doesn't look heavily used, and it's a little unusual in that it is right next to the trail. Usually there's a short side trail to these campsites. This site might be one of the lesser-used sites in the park. It's not extremely isolated, but it's not on the route to anything of significance to the typical visitor. A fisherman-backpacker might take this trail from Forney to Hazel Creek, but surely he wouldn't camp here. He'd camp on one of those main creeks, where the fish are. Most people probably use Poplar Flats the way I'm using it, as a rest stop to refill the water bottles, if they use it at all.

I arrived at the Welch Ridge Trail about 3 hours after leaving Melissa and John in camp. This portion of Welch Ridge is very easy, but I was only on it for about half a mile. As I began walking on Welch Ridge, I was hoping the trail to High Rocks would be well-marked and obvious. If I missed it, I would be alerted by Cold Spring Gap Trail which would be about half a mile past the High Rocks side trail. If I reached Cold Spring Gap, I'd just turn around and try again.

After a few minutes I changed my mind. I began to hope that the High Rocks side trail was obscure and poorly marked. Maybe the trail would be overgrown and the wooden sign would have rotted and washed away. After all, the point of this trip is to have this peak all to myself.

Well, no such luck. After a mere ten minute stroll on Welch Ridge, I came to the well-maintained side trail to High Rocks, marked with a solid wooden sign pointing the way. For about two seconds I considered hiding the sign and trail with leaves and branches, but my conscience intervened at the last second, as it occasionally does in moments of severe temptation. Hikers tend to be good, altruistic people. They love wilderness and solitude, but they tend to be accommodating of other hikers, too. Just one, big, happy family. That's why the sign was still standing there for me to see.

The hike to High Rocks was quick and easy. There was an interesting spot where a few stairs had been cut into some rocks.

There were shrubs growing in and around the steps, so it looked like part of an old, undiscovered Mayan temple.

A few yards beyond the rock stairs was the site (four concrete pads) of the old firetower and a deteriorating cabin with a large, blue tarp over the top of it. The tarp detracted from the wilderness feel, but I suppose you could say the same thing about the cabin. I hope that the tarp was a sign that the NPS was trying to save the cabin and would soon try to repair the rotting roof and floors. Nevertheless, the inside of the cabin was still partly intact. Windows, paint, and even a few old tools. Someone had taken an old metal chair out of the cabin and set it up on the exposed rocks next to the cabin. I'm thrilled and amazed that it's possible to find hidden jewels like this – old cabins that have not been ransacked by looters and defaced by vandals. And, yes, I'm pleased that no one hid the High Rocks sign back at the trail intersection. High Rocks is a good, lonely spot that belongs to all of us.

The view? Well, it's good, I suspect. This was, after all, the location of a firetower. But today thick clouds were speeding across the peak, so the visibility was about 30 feet. It would be a good view, weather permitting – but in the Smokies weather often does *not* permit. Even on a clear day, the view would not be 360°, but I can say with confidence that the trip was well worth the effort. A pleasant hike on a beautiful trail. A good variety of experiences – rivers, ridges, a fine view ("weather permitting"), an old cabin, mist, wind, and isolation. Like many of life's blessings, it's more than a guy like me deserves, but I'll gladly accept them when offered.

The seven miles back down to Forney were quick and easy. And quiet. It had been windy at High Rocks, but here on the eastern slope of Welch Ridge it was so serene and lonely that if a tree had fallen, it would *not* have made a sound, regardless of whether or not I had been there to hear it. The solitude caused me to stop several times to simply appreciate the fact that this is how it would have felt in October, 1491, or October, 3,000 BC. Same birds. Same clouds and fog, although a bit less acidic than now. Similar trees, but probably not the identical species – all the chestnuts are now gone, and the hemlocks are fading fast. Definitely the same quiet. That's the kind of stuff you think about when you are lucky enough to spend an entire day in the mountains without seeing another human being. Even if you aren't the contemplative type, the stillness and loneliness forces it on you, if for no other reason than there's nothing else to do.

The day had been devoid of wildlife, as hikes in the Smokies often are. I had seen a grasshopper and a couple of chickadees. That was it... until I spooked a wild boar (an exotic species that wouldn't have been here in 1491) that was standing beside the Bear Creek Trail about midway between Poplar Flats and Forney Creek. I'm glad I spooked him while we were still about 50' apart, because he sure spooked me. I've never had a bad encounter with a wild boar or a bear in the Smokies, but there's something about wild boars that gives me the heebie jeebies. Okay, actually it's not "something" that gives me the heebie jeebies – it's their tusks, and their muscles, and their fur. They are fierce looking. I know this is bordering on irrational, but I'd rather take my chances with a bear than a wild boar. Yeah, I know that bears will climb trees and eat other mammals, and as far as I know boars generally don't, but wild boars look like they'd kill you just for the fun of it. After all, toy companies make stuffed bears and call them Teddy Bears. You buy them for little kids to cuddle with. They don't make Teddy *Boars* for kids. In fact, the monsters in the closet of my childhood bedroom looked a lot like wild boars.

I've had only two previous wild boar encounters in the Smokies. One was a family of five in Cades Cove, a mother and four babies. As they trotted across the road in front of me, I wondered if the rangers would arrest me or reward me if I ran over them. I decided that even if they paid me for my act of community service, the money might not cover the cost of repairing my truck. The other sighting was last year at Forney Creek, close to the spot where my kayak was beached on this trip. Apparently Forney Creek is a good place to go if you want to see wild boar.

We parted company without incident, and I arrived back at the campsite exactly fourteen miles and seven hours after I had left it.

That evening at the campsite, the three of us were eating supper – cheese crackers, granola bars, water, and the added luxury of canned tuna – when Melissa saw a dark shape at the other end of the campsite, maybe 50 feet away. At first we thought it was a bear, but it didn't look quite right. It was backwards – the big, bulky end was in the front and the small end was at the rear. Although we could barely see it, we knew that it had to be a wild boar. A big, fierce, black wild boar rooting around, tearing up the ground like a power tiller. Was this guy following me? Would he visit me in my tent tonight?

I looked for a tree with low branches to climb in case of emergency, then we grabbed our cameras and moved closer to get some pictures. We each snapped a picture, but the flashes scared him away. I filed that bit of information in the "what to do in case of wild boar attack" section of my brain. In grizzly country people carry guns and pepper spray. In wild boar country, carry a camera with a flash. I took my camera to bed with me that night for protection – sort of a cross between a night light and pepper spray, to keep the real monsters away. If attacked I'd simply take the boar's picture.

A few days later, as I told my wife about our boar encounter, it occurred to me that there's another advantage of this camera defense – if the flash didn't scare the boar, at least she'd have a great picture of my killer, indisputable evidence that I died a noble death in the wilderness.

Assuming, of course, that being mauled and eaten by a pig qualifies as a noble death.

Chapter 2
Sixty-Eight Miles

Pilgrimage. For millennia the Jews have traveled to Jerusalem. For centuries Muslims have sojourned to Mecca. Hindus wash in the holy waters of the Ganges. Baseball fans attend a game at Wrigley Field. Football fans watch the Packers play at Lambeau Field (if they can get tickets). There are other pilgrimages for other sorts of people: Graceland, Wounded Knee, Sturgis, the Vietnam Memorial. For all these pilgrimages the purpose of the journey is to reach the holy site. It is the destination that makes the trip worth the travel.

Some people have described hiking the Appalachian Trail as a pilgrimage. I suppose they mean that hiking the AT is a wonderful, spiritual experience and completing its entire 2,181 miles is a great accomplishment. And it does *look* like a pilgrimage. Lots of dirty, haggard people, their belongings stuffed in and dangling from the packs strapped to their backs, walking with missionary zeal. But one important difference between a pilgrimage and hiking the AT is that in hiking the AT it is the journey itself, not the destination, that is most valuable. Making it to Mount Katahdin on the north end or Springer Mountain on the south is a challenge and an accomplishment, but *walking* there is more important than actually *arriving* there. In fact, I've seen hikers approaching the end of the AT on the top of Katahdin, sobbing uncontrollably because the greatest experience of their life was ending.

On a warm August afternoon many years ago, Allen and I stood on the dam which creates Fontana Lake out of the Little Tennessee River. The air was getting hotter by the minute and the heat waves rising from the concrete and the washed-out sky gave the impression that it would never be cool again, which of course wasn't true. Tonight we'd have our jackets on as we cooked supper at Birch Spring shelter, our first of seven nights in our 68 mile hike on the Appalachian Trail from this end of the Smokies to the northeastern end at Davenport Gap

"Howdy." The voice came from behind us. A middle-aged man and his wife, pasty white and significantly overweight approached. (This was in the olden days, before high fructose corn syrup and fast food had made *everyone* in America overweight.) "You look like you're heading somewhere."

"Into the park, up there." Allen pointed with his nose north across the dam and into the woods.

"Is there a trail, or are you bushwhackin'?" asked the man.

"A trail. The Appalachian Trail."

"Sounds nice."

We could tell from the "sounds nice" followed by an awkward silence that the man had no idea what the Appalachian Trail was. I wondered then, as I've wondered many times since, how any American can grow up into adulthood and not know what the AT is. I thought about asking the old man, but bless his heart, the guy was just trying to be friendly. So we both just nodded and said, "Yeah, it is."

Then the man added, "We've been in the mountains almost a week now. We've been to The Knife Works, Black Bear Jamboree.... Where else, Honey?"

His wife jumped in now that the conversation had shifted to familiar territory. "Dollywood, The Elvis Museum…"

The list might have continued, but I had stopped listening. "In the mountains." It's a seemingly straightforward phrase that means vastly different things to different people. In this couple's dictionary, it means going shopping and taking in a few shows. My dictionary takes the more literal meaning of, well, going to the *mountains*, as in: "It's been nice talking to you, but if you'll please excuse us, Allen and I are going to *the mountains*."

"At least they won't be in the park, cluttering up the trails," Allen muttered with a slight sense of superiority. Self-righteousness is probably the greatest sin of hikers simply because we have found a way to mix an appreciation of nature with physical exertion while at the same time rejecting the mass consumption and addiction to mindless entertainment that pervades our society. The Roman populace had bread and circuses. Americans have reality TV (an oxymoron if there ever was one), video games, and "shop 'til you drop." In fact, now that I've put that down on paper, it looks pretty convincing. Maybe we are superior.

As we walked across the dam I was struck by the beauty of the lake on one side and the river far below. "All this is man-made, but it really is beautiful," I commented. (This was during my 'wilderness is good, civilization is bad' phase, so admitting that a human-made scene was beautiful was a bold move on my part, maybe even blasphemous. I probably blushed as I said it.) But as we followed the white painted blazes into the woods, Allen added, "This will be better, if the next three hours don't kill us first." Then he adjusted a few straps, looked uphill and said with stoic resignation, "Well, it ain't gettin' done just standing here." He paused to adjust another strap and, without another word, began to walk.

And that's how these things get done. You don't dwell on the fact that this will be hard. You don't give each other a pep talk. You don't even give yourself a pep talk. You simply make sure your straps are secure, your boot laces are tied, and you do it. And at the end of the day, when you arrive at the top of your climb, you just sit down and say, "That was tough." And the other guy responds, "Yeah." And that's the end of it. At least that's the way we guys do it. Girls may be a bit more supportive and conversational, but for us boys there's really not much else to say. Your mission was to hike up a mountain trail, so you hiked up a mountain trail, and it was hard, just as you had expected. No self-respecting male would be caught dead giving words of encouragement to his hiking partner... unless, of course, his hiking partner is his wife, in which case encouragement is part of the job description.

So, these first few hours would be hard. We would climb 1,000 feet in the next mile with 40 pounds on our back, then continue ascending steadily, with a killer last quarter mile to Shuckstack ridge and its old firetower. We knew the drill: just put one foot in front of the other and don't think about how close or far we are from the destination. On these steep climbs I try to notice what's around me rather than dwelling on my faltering lungs, but that's easier said than done. Usually all I notice is the ground directly in front of me. There was only one way to get to the shelter and then the main crest – one step at a time.

In these mountains there are three main types of trails: those along rivers, which are the easiest because they follow the gradual gradient of the river; those along ridge crests, which have some significant climbs and descents but are manageable; and those ascending the side of a ridge, which usually involves strenuous climbs including numerous switchbacks. Climbing 500 to 600 feet in a mile is very common. Climbing 1,000 feet per mile is not unheard of. This first day was the "ascending the side of a ridge" type of hike. A rough way to start, but inevitable, and you get it over with early.

One interesting thing about a long, steady ascent is that you tend to do a lot of thinking, mainly because there's nothing else to do. You could talk to your partner, and occasionally you do, but on this type of hike breath is in short supply, so eventually talking gets reduced to a bare minimum. So you talk to yourself, silently in your head to preserve oxygen, and one of the questions that invariably gets asked, especially on a hard, uphill hike with no end in sight, is: Why am I doing this?

The answer to that question is different for different people, and it probably changes with age. I've heard people say they do it for the exercise, but that doesn't quite make sense to me simply because few people do serious hiking often enough to stay in shape. In fact, just the opposite is true – you have to stay in shape in order to hike. Hiking simply for the exercise is like going to the dentist because you like the magazines in the waiting room – it's nice, but it's not why you're there.

Many years ago, when I began hiking, I did it with a sense of military fervor born of an attraction to the mountains and a lethal level of testosterone. The point was to make a direct frontal assault on the mountains and to defeat them, giving me another notch on my sword. Of course, I was oblivious to the hardships of past generations of hikers who carried sixty pound packs, canvas tents, wool blankets, axes, and canned food. In comparison to them, all this talk about frontal assaults and conquest sounds like the barking of a Chihuahua.

Be that as it may, military conquest was my main purpose on this week-long trip on the AT, but another factor had begun creeping into my consciousness: peer pressure. There's a subtle difference between backpacking and becoming a backpacker. Backpacking is an activity that one engages in, but "becoming a backpacker" is making a commitment; it's adopting a new self-image. It's like the difference between attending church vs. experiencing a life-changing, religious conversion. When this conversion takes place, you find that your priorities, your reading material, your language, and your friends change. You think more about backpacking, you subscribe to outdoors magazines, and your circle of friends changes to include kindred, outdoor spirits. And these new friends become your new standard for judging your behavior and your accomplishments. When one of them asks about your hikes in the Smokies, you must be able to converse without hesitation about the entire length of the AT in the park. Phrases like Spence Field, Charlies Bunion, Tricorner Knob, and Shuckstack must fall from your lips as fluently as the words to your favorite song. Anything less brings scorn and shame from your new peers. In short, you must make this week-long hike just to hold up your end of the conversation, to be able to say that you've done it. It's not the most noble of motivations, but it's essential to maintaining your trail cred.

Of course, underlying all of this is a simple love of the mountains. Pretty much everyone appreciates a great view from a mountain. After all, there's a reason why people use the phrase "mountain top experience" to describe those life-changing events, after which things are never quite the same again. Moses isn't the only guy to have met God on a mountain top. But not everyone is thrilled with the prospect of *walking* to the top. As much sense as hiking makes to me, it doesn't make sense to everyone. A woman once asked me, "How can you just walk all day long?" My response wasn't a well-thought defense of my beloved pastime because I didn't have a well-thought defense. I just like hiking, so I opted for the short, blunt answer: "I don't know…. How can you go to the mall all day long?" Thus ending the conversation. As I recall, I thought I was funny, but she didn't, which is an enduring theme of my life.

It seems to me that if more people were lovers of the outdoors, we'd have a kinder, gentler world. On the other hand, while we kind and gentle folks were away, playing outside, the bad guys would probably end up running – and ruining – the world. Although, it sometimes feels like life is already headed in that direction, so maybe we missed our chance.

That first night at Birch Spring shelter I didn't sleep well because I never sleep well on the first night. On these trips I sleep soundly about every *other* night, starting with night #2 because the bunks are hard, my sleeping pad is thin, and my waded up clothes are a poor excuse for a pillow. By the second night I'll be absolutely exhausted, so sleep will force itself upon me.

As I lay there listening to the wind, I wondered if it always gets windy at night or was I finally calm enough to hear the noise that had been background music all day? The wind is such a common sound, and yet I rarely stop to listen to its music or to watch it work upon the trees. Lying in a shelter on the AT is the closest I ever get to hearing the Aeolian music as John Muir heard it that day in the top of a Douglas Fir. Maybe I've been too focused on having experiences in the wilderness, rather than experiencing the wilderness. Maybe that should change.

The next morning started cool, but dry. A perfect, summer, mountain day. In spite of all our uphill hiking yesterday, we were still not quite on the main ridge. Once we reached the main crest at Doe Knob, the hike became a 7 day stretch of ups and downs with great views, thick deciduous forest, exposed rock, mountain laurel and rhododendron thickets, spruce-fir forests, and grassy balds. The balds and exposed, rocky tops give a sense of being above the treeline, even though you are not. This far south the treeline would be about a thousand feet above our heads.

We hadn't seen many people yesterday and the shelter had been only half full, but today we saw more, going both ways. None were through-hikers, most of whom were probably in New Hampshire by now, maybe even in the Hundred Mile Wilderness of Maine.

The Smokies are such a revered location that you see quite a few people on this 68 mile stretch. You won't normally feel crowded, but you definitely are not isolated. This catches novices by surprise because they expect a howling, empty wilderness, but what they get on most of the 2,181 miles of the AT is a variety – some wilderness, some small towns, a few farms, and even an interstate highway or two. You see plenty of people, both hikers and trail-side residents. I don't know what the longest stretch of AT between paved roads is, but I suspect that the 38 miles from Fontana to Newfound Gap and the 31 miles from Newfound Gap to Davenport Gap are both in the top ten.

Most of the people you encounter on the AT are normal, well-adjusted folks, but there are a few screwballs and eccentrics. During the first few days of our week in the Smokies, Allen and I spent a couple of nights in shelters with a guy from England, who had quit his job and was taking a couple of years to wander around "the New World," as he called it. He'd recently traversed South America and the Pacific Crest Trail in California and was now hiking the AT, although probably not the entire AT because this was late August and he was still in the Smokies, heading north. If his goal was Katahdin, he was several months behind schedule and would arrive in Maine in December which would be really, really grim. Even if he didn't realize that yet, he'd surely have it figured out by October. I'm guessing he got about as far as New Jersey and then went to visit the Statue of Liberty before heading back to London. We envied him.

Then there were the two carpenters from Florida. They'd build houses about 5 months a year, November through March. The other 7 months were spent camping and backpacking, sometimes in the eastern US, sometimes out west. Seven months of free housing in shelters and tents, seeing the prettiest parts of the US. No health insurance, no families, no retirement plan, no permanent address, no long-term goals. They were being short-sighted and irresponsible, and we envied them for it, wishing we had the guts to be so free.

When you are out on the AT, you'll frequently run into young couples, maybe married, maybe not. Although you might think there would be some interesting stories that would emerge from this, there usually aren't. Generally, these young couples keep to themselves and don't have much to say to the rest of us. Occasionally you'd hear some giggles from their corner of the shelter late at night. Young couples always sleep in the corner away from the riff-raff. As a member of the riff-raff, I completely understand.

The most entertaining are the groups of local, college-age guys who know each other well and are hiking together. They laugh and joke late into the night. Occasionally their light-heartedness is enhanced by mind-altering substances, which often jump starts a song or two. When it's happening you feel like you've stumbled into Monty Python's Flying Circus, but with stout Southern accents. Every now and then one of them will pull out an obscure musical instrument, a harmonica being the most common, although on this particular occasion it was a ukulele. That evening in the Spence Field shelter, their rendition of *Stairway to Heaven* accompanied by a ukulele set a new standard for classic rock. Now whenever I hear that song, I am immediately transported to the Spence Field shelter, and I have them to thank for it.

About half the time, you'll have one hiker in the shelter who is just plain strange. I don't know why, but these guys almost always arrive late, after dark like possums or vampires. There are two types: the guys who don't speak at all to anyone and the guys who are eager to share their vast reservoir of experience with the rest of us, even if our body language is making it absolutely clear that we aren't interested in hearing it.

The quiet guys make you wonder what they are up to, but at least they aren't annoying. The talkative guys, however, can really get on your nerves. A talkative one showed up at the Spence Field shelter about two hours after sunset.

"Is this Russell Field? I lost my maps a week ago."

"No, this is Spe…"

"It doesn't matter. I've been out for 6 months. I've been in Colorado and Virginia and started at Big Creek two weeks ago. They let us through-hikers sleep wherever we want."

"Actually, this shelter is full. You're supposed to…"

"I'll just sleep here on the floor. You guys'll have to put your packs somewhere else." (Pause to take a breath and change subjects.) "You know, breathable jackets don't really breathe. It's physically impossible for the water vapor to escape."

At this point, no one is listening, and everyone has his back to the intruder. Most are busy putting on breathable jackets, which we wouldn't hike without. We all swear by them.

"I'm telling you, it's the biggest sham ever perpetrated by the backpacking apparel industry."

"Okay," I'm thinking, "I'm always willing to concede the point that public opinion is manipulated by Madison Avenue, not to mention the CIA, the Pentagon, and the New York Times, but if this guy mentions aliens..."

"It's alien technology that has a more sinister purpose. I'm presently doing research for my dissertation. I'm not in a grad program right now. Damn 'experts' don't respect the truth, but I'm on the verge of a breakthrough. You'll read about it when I publish my results."

I'm thinking how sorry I am that I let my subscription to *Mad Magazine* lapse; looks like I'll miss his exposé on the alien, breathable jacket conspiracy. Everyone else is thinking, "Don't make eye contact. Don't speak. It will only encourage him."

Everyone, that is, except one of the college guys who's still a little high, and a bit too daring. "I know what you mean, man. I was abducted by them bastards when I was four."

"Then you know of what I speak. They are up to something. That's why you've gotta stay on the move, off the grid, be random, they want you to be predictable and passive like sheep. The X-Files are real, man. Not the werewolves and vampires. The alien agenda."

I'm thinking, "I don't know exactly what the 'alien agenda' is, but I hope it involves taking this guy with them. Soon." It's at this point that I began thinking we normal ones should draw straws to determine who will stay awake all night standing guard. We never actually posted a sentry that night, but we all tried to stay awake until we were sure the guy had gone to sleep.

He was gone when we awoke in the morning. Someone asked, "Where's the Unabomber?" and we all got the joke.

"I saw a bright flash of light from the sky last night, and never saw him again. He's probably on Neptune by now."

"He must be glad to be home."

Our third day was a tough, up and down, 11.5 mile hike to Silers Bald shelter. During the day we saw a few guys hiking alone, which of course elicited some Unabomber jokes among us. I was glad our encounter with him happened early in the trip because it gave us something to talk about for the rest of the week. The topic of the Unabomber or the Ted Kaczynski School of Charm came up at least once a day.

Much of the main crest in the Smokies is deciduous forests, so you have only occasional views. But today's hike is mostly open fields and rocky, open peaks. It's a unique stretch of trail with a sense of being above timberline. One of the best spots on this section of the trail is Thunderhead, a rocky, open peak with fabulous views that you reach after a fierce 500 foot climb in less than half a mile.

We shared the peak of Thunderhead with one guy who had started out with a partner, but had now been hiking alone for two days. He had started with his friend in Damascus (on the TN–VA state line) and was heading south to Springer. His partner had made it as far as Newfound Gap and quit. They arrived at Newfound Gap, and his friend, who had thought it would be "cool to try backpacking" (that's a bad sign, a novice who doesn't grasp the magnitude of the challenge), sat down on the rock wall and refused to get up. He hitched a ride to Gatlinburg and went home.

In theory I have no problem with quitting. Quit smoking. Quit a lousy job. Quit whining. But the key is what you quit and why. Quitting because something isn't fun or is too hard is not copacetic, as is quitting on a commitment to another person. I won't say I've never quit something in those circumstances. I'm just saying that when it happens, people have a right to be disgusted with me. If they bad-mouth me, I deserve it, and I should take it like a man.

This guy had the right to criticize his ex-partner, but he didn't. He just told the story, and we all shook our heads sympathetically and drew our own conclusions about the cry-baby quitter. Although, in the quitter's defense, his biggest mistake wasn't in the quitting; it was in starting the trip in the first place. And besides, the guy on the trail was glad he was gone. I've never had a hiking partner bail out on me, but there are one or two that I wish had.

Several years ago a journalist wrote a New York Times bestseller about "walking in the woods." (I'm trying to keep this semi-anonymous, but that was a hint.) Maybe you've read the book and enjoyed it. He's a good writer, and he wrote well about his experiences in hiking the AT. In my opinion, the most amazing thing about his trip is that he and his partner got fed up with the rain and the dirt and the "dingy rock shelters" in the Smokies, so they quit at Newfound Gap, rode to Gatlinburg, ate some expensive hamburgers, caught a taxi to Knoxville, then drove to Roanoke, VA. They skipped the eastern half of the Smokies, all of Tennessee, and much of Virginia! I was so disgusted that I quit reading. I don't know how the book ends, but I hope at some point they came to grips with the reality that if you hike the AT, you are going to get wet and dirty, and the accommodations are somewhat primitive.

On the other hand, I have to admit that they did something that I've never done. No, not hiking the entire AT, since they didn't. I'm talking about heading out into the woods without seeing the light at the end of the tunnel. And I do envy them for that. Every backpacking trip I've ever taken has had a clearly defined beginning and end. What would happen in the middle was not always clear when I started, but I always knew that "next Saturday I'll hike back to the car and go home." I could see that light at the end of the tunnel, and I hated it. To step into the woods thinking, "I'm not sure when and where this is going to end," must be an adrenaline rush that very few of us get to experience. Unfortunately, the closest most of us ever get to this "no end in sight" feeling is being trapped in a job we hate but can't quit; or, hearing the good news that this year's Federal budget deficit is only 500 billion dollars, rather than the 750 billion that was originally projected. Sorry, I can't think of any happy examples.

We heard grunting and snorting all night long outside the Silers Bald shelter, but we were safely embedded in our rock shelter with a chain link fence and gate across the front. The animal noises were good background music, and we slept well.

Our fourth day was another tough up and .... Okay, let's stop for a second. Because we had over 30 pounds of gear and food strapped to our backs, and because this main ridgecrest is a long string of peaks and gaps, and because the trail blazers sent the trail *over* most peaks rather than skirting *around* them, most days were tough, up and down, hikes; so I'll quit saying it. We're both probably getting tired of hearing it.

As we approached Clingmans Dome (the highest point on the entire AT, 6,625 feet), the deciduous forest switched to spruce and fir. Although in recent years these forests have been gradually receding due to insect pests (and maybe heat and acid rain), they were still there back when we made this hike and were still enchanting. You are overwhelmed by the *green*. The deciduous forests are green, too, but these spruce-fir forests are just... *different*. They seem cooler, shadier, and greener. Deeper. Maybe *Canadian* is the word I'm looking for because all the guidebooks tell you that this last, lingering stand of conifers is the type found in New England and Canadian forests. But it's more than just a deep, cool green. There's an element of magic to it. Stepping into a spruce-fir forest is like stepping through the wardrobe door and into Narnia.

While the views from Clingmans Dome are fine, there were crowds of people, so we didn't even walk the extra hundred feet to the top of the spiral, concrete tower. Instead, we just walked below it as we passed. The views there are fabulous on a cool, crisp day, but on a typical August day you'll see mostly haze from humidity mixed with pollution. That's the case throughout the park, so if you want really incredible views, come when the weather has cooled a bit.

When you are backpacking, your ego gets a boost when you walk out of the woods and into a crowd of tourists, such as at Clingmans Dome or Newfound Gap. You don't stop traffic as completely as a bear would, but you do rank up there with deer and foxes. Little children point and adults stare as you pass by, self-sufficient, carrying in your pack all you need to survive a week in the woods.

There have been numerous times that I've seen, out of the corner of my eye, people taking pictures of us as we sit in the grass, reclining against our packs. It's our 15 minutes of fame. If only our wives and girlfriends could see how much we are respected and feared by these complete strangers. It's at times like these that all that stuff I've said about communing with nature becomes irrelevant or just disappears altogether. It's just good to be one tough dude in someone's eyes for a few minutes, even if it's not really true. After half a week of backpacking, even a harmless guy like me doesn't *look* harmless.

After spending our fourth night at the Mt. Collins shelter, Allen and I cruised down to the Newfound Gap parking lot where the main road crosses the main crest. There we met Frank and Joey who would finish the eastern half of the park with us. They had arrived a day earlier and had hiked on one of the park's other trails to a backcountry camp site. They had slept there in their tent and had then hiked out and driven up to meet us.

Because the AT is the matriarch of America's system of national trails, there's a certain mystique in expending some time and energy on it. On the other hand, there are over 750 miles of non-AT trails in the Smokies. Near the roads, these trails can have some small crowds on them. Deeper in, you'll see very few people even in the peak summer tourist season. One nice aspect of these backcountry trails is that there's a little more sense of *wandering* in the woods. On the AT, you are on the main crest and your route is pre-determined, and you must stay in the rock shelters which must be reserved a month in advance. On the web of backcountry trails, there are numerous intersections and side trails to explore and many simple, isolated campsites. Of course, in the park you can't wander aimlessly. You have to make reservations ahead of time to let the rangers know which campsites you'll be staying in. The paperwork of the federal bureaucracy reaches even into the depths of the Smokies wilderness. Nevertheless, you do have more options in the non-AT backcountry.

My backpacking log book tells me that I have backpacked about 40 nights and 260 miles on the AT, from Springer Mountain, GA, to the eastern end of the Smokies. I've also backpacked about 50 nights and 350 miles in the Smokies' non-AT, backcountry trails. I just remembered that I have also day hiked the northernmost 5 miles of the AT up to the top of Mt.

Katahdin in Maine, so I have a picture of me standing not only on Springer Mountain at the southern end but also on Mount Katahdin at the northern end. Maybe I'll display the two pictures in a prominent place in my home and let my guests assume what they will about the 2,181 mile gap in between. Who am I to correct their mistaken impression? Pictures don't lie… except when they do.

Things are a little different outside the national park. The four of us once spent a week in Shining Rock Wilderness area, about an hour south of the Smokies on US 276. On that trip, we carried tents because there were no shelters. There were established trails and some campsites, but for the most part we were unhindered. We didn't have to pre-arrange our itinerary with any rangers. We just hiked when and where we wanted to go. We mostly stayed on trails, but we did do some map and compass off-trail hiking that was a lot of fun. This kind of carefree wandering is something that you can't quite do in the Smokies. It's still legal to hike off the trails in the Smokies, but you have to end up spending the night in an established campsite or shelter.

The four of us spent our fifth night in our old friend, Icewater Spring shelter. I've spent more nights in the Smokies in this shelter than anywhere else in the park. It's also the park's most heavily-used shelter because it's only a three mile hike from Newfound Gap, and it can serve as a gateway to a nice hike up Mt. Le Conte or to Charlies Bunion. We slept well that night. Eventually…

When Allen started screaming, my response was to hunker down deeper in my sleeping bag, hoping that whatever was killing him would not notice me. After a few seconds I heard Joey talking to him, calming him down. At that point, I realized, through the fog of sleep, that we were not being killed and eaten by a bear, aliens, or the Unabomber. It was one of Allen's nighttime episodes. I had heard that he sometimes would wake up at night screaming, but I hadn't experienced it until that night at Icewater Spring. Allen had been my most consistent backpacking partner during that period in my life, but it was times like this that I wondered if maybe we should have put each other through an application process. Question 1: Have you ever backpacked before? (Because you don't want to babysit your backpacking partner.) Question 2: How fast can you run? (Because you don't have to outrun a bear; you only have to outrun your hiking partner.) Question 3: Do you ever wake up screaming in the middle of the night? (Because no one likes a wet sleeping bag.) Nevertheless, we made it through the night just fine.

I enjoy these three-sided rock and mortar shelters. Some folks call them dirty and dingy. I call them rustic and quaint. Not in an antique shop way, more of an old barn way. They have been heavily used for many years, so they show some wear and tear, but even the wear and tear is a reminder that you are doing something that people have been doing for several generations, and people will continue to do it long after you are gone. You are a link in a long chain of main crest hikers. It's enough to tempt you to carve your name on the old log rafters for future generations to see, a temptation that a lot of people yield to, but I am able to resist. Other than the fact that it's a federal misdemeanor, I guess I'm holding on to the hope that my legacy to future generations will consist of a little more than "Greg loves Phyllis" or "Wet Dog Trillium was here." (I don't have a hiking moniker, but if I did it would be Wet Dog Trillium – a Smokies, spring wildflower that smells like a wet dog and is also known as Stinking Benjamin.)

These old shelters are rustic, solid, and secure. Well, they were secure on this trip several years ago. Today there's no front on them, but for many years there was a chain link fence and gate across the front to keep out the bears, which was important because we hikers would hang our food in bags from the rafters. The mice loved it.

There were two approaches to dealing with the mice: deterrence and acquiescence. The deterrence approach entailed using a plastic or metal lid with a small hole punched in the middle. You would slide the lid onto the rope holding your food bag from the rafters. Except for the case of unusually acrobatic mice, the critters couldn't get all the way down the rope to the food bag. This approach usually worked, but when it didn't you'd end up with holes chewed in your food bag and in your packets of gorp, milk powder, noodles, and cheese.

Acquiescence meant forgoing the lid and just leaving your food bag exposed and open, like going through customs in a third world country. You'd leave a little "gift" in your luggage for the inspector, and he'd let you in. The mice in the shelters operated in the same fashion. You cooperate, the mice get their small share, and everyone parts as friends in the morning.

I finally settled on a combination of the two approaches. I'd use the lid on the rope, but I'd keep my food bag open. If the mouse made it past the lid, he'd have easy access to my food bag, and I'd end up with a corner of my gorp bag chewed but no holes in my food bag. Not a high price to pay, as long as the mouse didn't get mad about the lid on the rope and exact his revenge while I slept.

Sometime during the night the skunks would make their entrance. They'd usually just wander around looking for food scraps, and when they were finished, they'd leave by whatever hole they had entered. Only once did I ever have to get up and let a skunk out the front gate because he couldn't find his way out. It was no different than letting the cat out at night, except the skunk showed some gratitude, something a cat would never condescend to do. I respect the danger and mystery of truly wild animals, but I could learn to love a well-mannered skunk.

In recent years the National Park Service has changed its policy. There are now high cables outside every shelter suspended between trees or metal poles. You hang your bags on these cables so bears, raccoons, skunks, and mice can't get them. These cables don't look mouse-proof to me, but apparently the mice haven't figured out what's going on because they don't seem to get into the food bags hung high on these outside cables. Maybe they are afraid of heights. These are, after all, field mice, not tree mice, right? I have no idea why squirrels haven't cracked the code. For whatever reasons, the cables do their job.

The main problem now is rain on your food, so you must use a waterproof bag for your food or just cover your bag with your rain jacket. Even so, I always hope it rains at night because one of the greatest sounds in the world is rain on a tin roof, which all these rock shelters have. A rainy night in a tin-roofed shelter on the crest of the Smokies is a simple, delightful experience; just one more compelling bit of evidence that Thoreau was right: "That man is richest whose pleasures are the cheapest."

The NPS's rationale for removing the fences across the front of the shelters was to enhance the wilderness experience, and in my opinion, it has. But even more importantly, it is a refreshing step back into the past. If you think about the overall trend of our society toward litigation, disclaimers, and bureaucratic rule-proliferation, this move by the NPS is an astounding, unprecedented step *backwards*, in the right direction. It's the only example I can recall of a major government or corporate institution bucking the trend of more stupid rules to protect us from ourselves. You've heard all the stories – lawsuits over hot coffee and slippery floors. Don't swim here. Don't run there. Don't try this at home. Professional stunt drivers on a closed course. While eating almonds recently, I looked on the back of the can, and I noticed a warning. It said, and I quote, "Allergy Warning: Contains almonds." Yeah, thanks for exposing that hidden threat. I guess the corporations and lawyers think we're a nation of idiots – or greedy pigs who will sue an almond company for putting almonds in a can of almonds without a warning. A few of us probably are that greedy or stupid, so the rest of us have to put up with being treated like morons. Welcome to modern life.

Take a moment and try to think of any change in the last 30 years that knowingly *increases* risk. Imagine… opening up a shelter, risking the possibility that a bear might enter! Whoever had this idea should be identified, named publicly, and have her face carved onto Mount Rushmore. She would get my vote for president. I hope she's still working for the National Park Service, but I'm afraid she probably has trouble keeping a job because she just doesn't fit in with the prevailing government or corporate culture. Maybe the NPS is a bastion of sanity in Washington, but that's not something that we can expect to last forever.

If you are worried about bears, take a couple of rocks or a stout walking stick to bed with you because now there's no fence to protect you. You can throw the rocks at any bears that show up, or just bop him on the nose with your stick. He'll get the point. But don't put any food in your sleeping bag. Let's delay the inevitable as long as possible – warning signs in these shelters, restating the obvious: "Warning: Bears are attracted to food." Of course, anyone who hasn't figured that out by now will probably be removed from the gene pool by a hungry bear anyway, so the problem will correct itself through natural selection whereby the clueless are eliminated by the hungry.

That night at Icewater Spring, behind the chain link fence, we were visited by mice and skunks, but no bears. But it did rain, which was perfect percussion music for sleeping, which we finally did… when all the screaming stopped.

The next morning we awoke to rain and mud. That's often the price you pay for the soothing sound of rain on your shelter's tin roof. It rained all day on our 12 mile walk to Tricorner Knob shelter. I almost wrote, "*Unfortunately*, it rained all day…." But you know, nature's gotta do what nature's gotta do, and in the Smokies, nature's gotta rain. A lot. We'd been rained on several afternoons so far on this trip, but this was the first day that it would rain from morning to evening. We were clearly going to get wet, again.

I had two T shirts (one wet and one dry), two pairs of shorts (one wet and one dry), two pairs of socks (one wet and one dry), one pair of sweat pants (still dry), and a wool shirt. My big decision for the day was: wet clothes or dry? I went with wet.

If it's raining, you can try to stay dry or you can just give in. I just gave in and hiked wet because I didn't want to risk getting to tonight's shelter with absolutely no dry clothes. I put on my wool shirt (a magical fiber that doesn't absorb water and keeps you warm even when wet) over my wet clothes, which were cold, kept my dry clothes in my pack, and began hiking. Today hikers use polyester fleece and Gore-Tex instead of wool, but this trip was in the 20th century when we sometimes wore materials that came from animals rather than petroleum.

I know hypothermia is always a risk in wet weather, but between the strenuous walking, constant snacking, and my wool shirt, I was fine. With a wool shirt or a waterproof, breathable jacket, it's possible to actually dry out your wet clothes that you are wearing while hiking in the rain. So, I was warm, toasty, and dry, thanks to an old, army surplus wool shirt. I don't know where that shirt is today, but I miss it dearly and speak fondly of the good times we had together.

This was also the day I had my sugar and meat conniption. I had planned my food so that I ate the same thing every day. Breakfast was granola bars and chocolate (powdered) milk, lunch – the meal you eat all day long between breakfast and supper – consisted of cheese crackers, raisins, and peanuts. For supper I'd have a couple of packets of dried chicken noodle stew – just add boiling water. I had intentionally omitted candy. Same routine every day. That was a mistake.

By the sixth day I was obsessing about... well, the list would be long. Let's just say I was obsessing about *everything except* the food I had in my pack: granola bars, powdered milk, cheese crackers, raisins, peanuts, and dried chicken stew. I really wanted some chocolate candy and a Coke, but when we stopped for a break at Pecks Corner shelter to rest and get out of the rain, what I really, really wanted was the big sausage log that another hiker was eating. Murder was out of the question. Too many witnesses. Robbery was an option, but I'd never actually robbed anyone before, so I wasn't real confident that I could pull it off. Sleight of hand might work, but he wouldn't lay that sausage down. He protected it like a mama bear protects her cub, never letting it out of his sight. He could probably see the virulent case of sausage-lust in my eyes.

During the conversation in the shelter we discovered that he and his partner had just started at our destination, Davenport Gap, the day before. They were spending a week on the AT, going the opposite direction from us. That meant offering to trade food with him was out of the question. First of all, all I had was junk. Powdered milk, cheap cheese crackers, raisins. If he had traded a couple of slices of his meat stick for some of my food, it would have been a clear case of babysitting on his part. I just couldn't lower myself to ask. I'd been self-sufficient all week, and I didn't want to give in now and have other people start taking care of me. Second of all, he was just starting on his trip. You just can't ask a guy to give up some of his prized food possessions that early on the trip. Near the end of a trip, backpackers willingly give up food they won't need, just to lighten the load, but not at the beginning. So, I just sat there and burned with desire for some smoked sausage. I know man doesn't live by bread alone, but right then a bite of sausage would have been heavenly.

In my defense, I thought about trading for the meat *before* I considered murder and robbery which would have been used only as last resorts, if at all. A week in the woods hadn't destroyed *all* my scruples, but they were in a weakened state regarding meat products.

Our arrival at Tricorner Knob prompted our usual routine. Claim a bunk, some prefer top, others prefer bottom. Find the spring and get water, usually 50 or 100 yards down one side or the other, a well-worn trail showing the way. Sit around or even take a quick nap before supper. Some guys carry a pair of sneakers to put on now. I didn't because of the extra weight, but I seriously consider it every time I backpack. If this trip had been shorter, I might have included them, but an extra couple of pounds were a lot to carry for a week. Now that we were at the evening's shelter, I burned with desire for my partners' shoes. Apparently, this was just a good day for coveting my neighbor's stuff. Again in my defense, I'm pretty sure that was the only one of the Ten Commandments I broke that day. For me, that's a pretty good day.

We saw our only bear of the week at Tricorner. He came during the night, stood and leaned against the fence at the front of the shelter, and shook it. We all woke up and watched for a few minutes, then he walked away into the darkness. We slept soundly until morning, letting the mice and skunks roam at will. At least we had finally seen a bear.

The following morning I awoke at daybreak to the sound of chirping, squawking birds. I hadn't noticed this level of bird activity any other mornings of our week, so I just lay there and listened. Then the bear showed up again, being severely scolded by the birds but taking it all in good humor. I know black bears will occasionally maul or kill a hiker, but my encounters with them have always been peaceful, even pleasant. They seem like such affable creatures… especially when they are on the other side of a protective fence.

He repeated his performance from that night, then left. We scrambled for our cameras, but didn't get them out in time. Everyone else went back to sleep, while I lay there reading whatever cheap paperback book I had brought with me for the week. (I'd burn the pages after I read them, to lighten my load.) After a few minutes, the birds sounded their alarm again, so I got my camera ready. The bear came for his encore. He stood and shook the gate, I snapped the only picture of the only bear sighting for the week, he left, and I continued reading. End of story. If you were hoping for an exciting bear-encounter story, you'll have to read a Yellowstone or Glacier grizzly story. Sorry. Now, mice stories. Ooohhh, I could tell you some mice stories... stories of deceit, theft, revenge, even one or two instances of tragic, bloody deaths.

We lazed around and didn't leave the shelter until almost 11 am, about two hours later than usual. The hike today was *not* tough. It was mostly high and level, and less than 8 miles. Our pace was leisurely which afforded us the opportunity to relax and carefully observe our surroundings which consisted of a nice spruce-fir forest on Mt. Guyot, beech gaps, drunk bees on Filmy Angelica, and impressive piles of purple poop.

The piles of bear crap (even a novice scatologist could see that piles of that magnitude could only come out of bears) were purple from the berries that were in season. We were drawn to one particularly imposing pile, still soft and warm with lots of tiny seeds, probably blackberry. We were the first to arrive on the scene. The perpetrator had narrowly escaped unseen; even the flies had not arrived yet. We gathered around it, admiring its form and content, convinced that the bear that created this masterpiece was the lord of this domain and was not to be messed with.

Native Americans could sometimes track animals by noting the direction the animal's turds were pointing. I suppose that means some animal scat has a pointy end that is produced, I assume, as the animal pinches it off. The turd falls to the ground pointing the direction of travel like a brown "One Way" sign. I would also assume that this system only works for animals that excrete while they walk, or at least start walking before they are finished. This particular pile that had attracted our attention was a deep, round mound with a little twist at the top like soft serve ice cream. It was obviously the work of a creature that was in no hurry and understands the value of a long, luxurious – and stationary – poop. In this respect, bears and I are kindred spirits. We understand one another.

This day, our seventh, was quiet and thoughtful. The hike was easy, so we weren't focused on the pain and sweat. The clouds were breaking up, and we had some nice views. We were in no hurry, so we made a lot of rest stops, even though we didn't need the rest. We were easing into that end-of-the-trip mode of reflection and sadness. Our last night at Cosby Knob was uneventful. It felt like the trip was finished, but it wasn't quite.

On our final morning, the reality of schedules reared its ugly head. A couple of our wives were to pick us up on Highway 32 in Davenport Gap at 3 pm, so we couldn't tarry. We left the shelter by 8:45 and soon began a steady ascent. The best part about today was the *lack* of views. Forests mixed with clouds made the panoramic views few and far between. This forced us to make the brief side trip to Mt. Cammerer in search of one last panorama. None of us had ever been there before, nor did we know much about it.

It turned out to be the highlight of the trip, which seemed appropriate. Allen and I had ascended about 19,000 feet (matched by 16,000 feet of descent) since our start at Fontana. After leaving Cammerer our hike would be all downhill, so this was a literal highpoint of sorts, even though it wasn't the actual highest point on our trip.

Mount Cammerer was great, and it's been great the dozens of times I've been there since this first encounter. It was love at first sight, and it's a love that has endured. Cammerer serves as the grandstand for the eastern end of the park, providing magnificent views in all directions, some in the park, some out. The fact that there's a unique, rock-and-wood lookout tower built in the 1930s by the CCC adds to its mystique.

We spent 45 overwhelming minutes there. The clouds had broken and risen. There were clouds above us, patches of fog in the valleys, and streaks of sunshine spotlighting the mountains and valleys. We took out our maps and compasses and identified several landmarks: English Mountain, the Big Creek watershed, Mount Sterling, Interstate 40 winding its way through the hills, Douglas Lake. I didn't know it at the time, but ten years later I would be living in those hills just past Douglas Lake.

Sometimes there *are* happy endings: Mt. Cammerer was a grand finale, we met our wives at Davenport Gap as planned, and my wife and I eventually moved to east Tennessee, an hour away from Big Creek, Cosby, and trails to Mt. Cammerer.

As I write this many years later, I have backpacked the southernmost 230 miles of the AT, from Springer Mountain in Georgia through the Smokies to Davenport Gap. I started in 1975 and finished in 2008. That's 33 years to walk 230 miles. Not a torrid pace – about 2 hundredths of a mile per day. At this rate, I should finish the remaining 1,951 miles in about 267 more years, so I'm beginning to think that I might not get it done.

But that's fine. Sure, I'd like to be able to say that I've walked the entire AT, but if you are looking for peace, beauty, and a sense of connection with the natural world, then you don't have to walk the entire length. Walking a mile with the right attitude is adequate. Although, I'd have to say that there is something extra to be gained by staying out on the trail for an extended period of time. There is a sense of intimacy that you can get by staying out for a week or two that can't be gotten by taking a 1 mile hike. Just as it takes time to build a relationship with another person, it takes time to build it with the natural world, and the fewer interruptions the better. Think of it as a vacation to reconnect with the spouse you've been neglecting.

I've spent a week backpacking in the Smokies a couple of times, and it's been my experience that in hiking the AT, the whole is definitely greater than the sum of its parts. Spending 7 days in a row on the AT is a very different experience from spending 7 separate days, scattered over several months or years. Hiking the entire AT in one long walk lasting 3 to 6 months is a very different experience than hiking the entire AT in small pieces scattered over several years. The lengthy immersion is the difference. It's what makes the one experience different from the other. An overnight hike is better than a day hike. A weekend trip is better than an overnighter. A week is better than a weekend. I guess at some point the law of diminishing returns kicks in, so that 36 days may not be significantly better than 35. I'll let you figure out at what point it would happen for you, but it's probably longer than a week.

Staying out several days or weeks enables you to get past the "Gee, this sure is pretty" stage and into the "What have I gotten myself into?" stage. You can't do that on a quick day hike, or even a one-nighter. If you stay out long enough, you'll get past those and move into the "Okay, I think I am going to survive this" stage. Hopefully, you'll get beyond that to the "I would love a hot shower and a cheeseburger, but I really don't want this to end" stage. That's the stage you want to end with, like the old rule that you should end a party while everyone is still having fun.

For some people there's probably a final, "Are we there yet?" stage; although, I don't know that for sure because we never reached that point. In fact, in the entire week I never heard that phrase uttered. Instead, we were still having fun when the party ended.

Chapter 3
Ridges and Rivers

We were on the Boulevard trail leading from the Appalachian Trail to the top of Mount Le Conte, and I had never been colder. I was a novice backpacker in my early 20s, and while I wasn't completely ignorant, I still didn't know the nuances of winter backpacking – such as, carbohydrates are as important as clothing; cotton is worthless when wet; and moisture from sweat is just as wet as moisture from rain and snow. I don't think GoreTex had been invented yet, but even if it had, I probably wouldn't have understood what all the excitement was about, but even if I did, I couldn't have afforded it. In fact, I still can't afford it, but now I buy it anyway. My kids can pay for their own college education.

My feet had been numb since the previous evening at Icewater Spring shelter, and they were still numb as my three hiking partners and I waded through calf-deep snow toward the top of Mt. Le Conte. I was wearing blue jeans and leather boots and had plastic bread bags on my feet over my socks, thinking they would keep my socks and feet dry. This was the trip on which the realities of sweat, condensation, cotton, and cold temperatures all became clear to me. I was the mule and the wet pants, socks, and feet were the 2 x 4 that finally got my attention.

We were all under-prepared (partly from lack of good sense, partly from lack of money) and miserable, but of course that simply reminded us of how masculine we all were, so it was well worth it. In fact, we were all so thoroughly miserable that we made this an annual event. With each passing year we'd each add to our stock of winter equipment, until after five or six years we finally had enough of the right stuff to keep us warm and dry, but not necessarily comfortable. And so, this route came to be called The Le Conte Trip, fully deserving of the capital letters.

It's good to have a working vocabulary, a short-hand code that emerges among friends with common interests and experiences. Every fall, as we'd begin thinking ahead to winter, one of us would simply say "Le Conte?" and we all knew exactly what he meant: not only the destination but also the number of days, the route, and the precise weekend. A wealth of information and memories were encapsulated in that one phrase. We'd occasionally try a different trip, but we kept coming back to The Le Conte Trip. It was just too good to not do. We repeated this adventure several more times until life's obligations (including a marriage, a divorce, a new career, and a deadly illness) separated our little backpacking fraternity.

So, for the next several Januarys we'd park at Newfound Gap and hike 3 miles to Icewater Spring shelter for the first night. Before going to bed for the night, we would hike the one mile to Charlies Bunion and scramble around on the rocks, enjoying the view and basking in the knowledge that we were all manly, outdoor types who were just a little superior to all those sissies in hotels in Gatlinburg.

The problem with winter backpacking is not just the cold. It's the early bedtime. That might sound like a good thing, but it's not. Depending on the cloud cover, it gets dark around 5 or 6 pm, and it's generally too cold to sit around and talk or play cards. (There's virtually no legal firewood around these backcountry shelters, so a decent fire was usually out of the question.) By 6 pm you are in your sleeping bag, eating gorp (good ol' raisins & peanuts) to stoke your metabolism, and praying that morning will come soon. It never does.

The bunks are hard. Your face sticking out of your sleeping bag is cold. And then you realize you didn't drink enough during the day. You reach down around your feet to dig out your water bottle. You keep it in your sleeping bag so it won't freeze. You drink and eat gorp and then drink some more. Then, just as you are thawing out, you have to pee.

Most folks just get up and pee. A few others somehow wait until morning. There's even a theory out there that your body uses more calories keeping the urine in your bladder at 98.6

degrees than it does to get up, walk out of the shelter, stand in the snow, pee, get chilled in the process, and crawl back into your bag and try to get warm by doing isometrics. As the theory goes, calorie-wise and warmth-wise, you should get up and pee. Personally, I believe that debate fills a much needed gap in the literature of backpacking. I just haven't reached that level of insight and sophistication, so I follow the same rule that I follow in my non-backpacking life: when you need to pee, go pee. Philosophers would call this Ockham's Razor; the rest of us call it Common Sense: when nature calls, you should answer.

One of my friends carries an extra bottle to pee in at night, so he won't have to get out of his sleeping bag. It's bright red and has a skull and crossbones drawn on it, so it looks a lot like those stickers you see on the back of trucks that are transporting hazardous materials. Of course, this means I must never, NEVER bring a red water bottle on a camping trip with him because the consequences of accidentally switching red bottles would be utterly unspeakable... except that it wouldn't be unspeakable. The story would be spoken among my hiking partners... and among their children, and among their children's children unto the seventh generation. It would immediately plunge me to the very bottom of the carefully constructed, male pecking order that exists among us. I may be at the bottom already, but that kind of blunder would cement my position there permanently with no hope of recovery.

Anyway, morning never comes... and I have proof. One year I went to bed at dusk and just couldn't get warm. I tossed and turned and struggled all night, dozing fitfully, keenly aware of every chilled body part. Finally, after a long, restless night I awoke to the sound of voices. Two of my partners were standing at the head of the bunks, discussing the impending uphill hike to Mt. Le Conte. My spirits soared. I had survived the long, cold night! I began to crawl out of my bag to eat breakfast. It seemed a bit dark, but I had been in my sleeping bag for 12, maybe 13, hours, and I was ready to get going. That's when I noticed that these guys were taking their boots *off*. I watched in horror as they unzipped their sleeping bags and crawled *in*. They were going to bed! It was 8:30 pm, and I had been in my sleeping bag about 2 hours. Morning hadn't come, and as best I can remember, it never did.

That all happened at the Icewater Spring shelter. The next day we hiked on the Boulevard trail to Mt Le Conte, where we spent the second night. There's a cozy lodge on top of Mt. Le Conte with a central dining hall, fireplace, and sitting area. There are several small cabins with beds, mattresses, pillows, and linens. Supplies are carried in by both ends of the technology spectrum: helicopters and lamas. It's not luxurious, but it's rustic and comfortable. And, most importantly, it's *not* where you stay on a backpacking trip to Le Conte.

Backpackers stay in a three-sided rock and mortar shelter with hard wooden bunk beds. Did you catch the part about three sides? The front is open to the elements, and in January in the Smokies there are some serious "elements," cold wind being at the top of the list, right above snow, moisture, and skunks. Of course, that's why you are backpacking in the Smokies in January. You are doing it to prove something to yourself, to your backpacking partners, and to your frail acquaintances back home. They don't have what it takes. You do. At least, that's what you keep telling yourself. Otherwise, sleeping in the cold and snow on top of a mountain in January begins to seem like a stupid idea.

Mount Le Conte is a big, dominant mountain covered mostly by virgin forest. It's either the tallest mountain in the park, or the third tallest, depending on how you want to measure it. If you start at sea-level, it's the third tallest at 6,593 – that's 50 feet shorter than Clingmans Dome. If you start at the base of the mountain, it's the tallest, rising 5,300 feet from its base. In fact, measured this way, it's the tallest mountain in the eastern US. Whenever I'm on the top of Le Conte, it doesn't bother me that two other mountains in the park are higher than I am. If you are the obsessive-compulsive type then such details might keep you awake at night, so you'd be better off driving to Clingmans Dome and making the half mile hike on the paved trail (along with the hundreds of other people) to the top, just to say you've been on the highest mountain in the park. And, of course, try not to think about the fact that there are two other peaks in the eastern US *outside* the park that are taller than Clingmans Dome.

Le Conte is about 34 miles south of my present home, as the crow flies. I can't see it from my house, but there are several locations nearby from which it is clearly visible. Or, I should say, it's clearly visible on a cool, crisp, clear day. From May through September the air is usually too warm and hazy to see it, but during cool weather it stands in the distance as a pleasant reminder that life is still good because there are mountains nearby. Viewed from the north, it has a distinctive shape to it – a broad, ridgetop over 1 mile long with four distinct humps on the highest ridge. Those humps are West Point, Cliff Top, High Top, and Myrtle Point, some of which have been popular spots to watch sunrises or sunsets for a hundred years.

To tell you the truth, on our winter trips I rarely walked to one of those points to see a Le Conte winter sunrise or sunset, partly because I was cold and tired, partly because I had explored Le Conte's ridgetop during other seasons, but mainly because winter hiking in the Smokies provides so many great views, I just didn't feel the need to walk to one of Le Conte's extremities to see another. I'd have been doing it just to say I'd done it, and that's something I quit doing when I realized that I wasn't going to do anything in life so rare and fabulous that I'd be able to impress folks with the tale of my achievement. Now I just hike or fish or whatever if it's something that I'll enjoy or learn from.

Besides, all the really good stuff has already been done – first man on the moon, first person to climb Everest, first person to hike the entire AT. Just thumb through a Guinness Book of World Records to see all the stupid, pointless activities that people are pursuing, just to say they've done it – balancing spinning plates on poles, eating hot dogs, etc. Did you know that a guy ate 36 cockroaches in less than one minute to break the old record? While it does add an interesting twist to the idea of a midnight snack, I wonder how you practice for something like that. Even more, I wonder why people would care, but apparently they do, which is one more reason to lament the future.

After our night on Le Conte, we always hiked back down to the main road via Alum Cave Trail. My favorite part is that it's all down hill. My second favorite part is the sections of trail that are simply cut into a vertical cliff. Hand cables are bolted into the rock, the trail is about four feet wide, and the drop-off to your right is sudden. It's awesome, if you don't slip on the ice that inevitably covers it in January. No, actually that's precisely what makes it awesome. Just be sure to wear crampons and don't let go of the cable.

Also awesome are the views from Le Conte, from Charlies Bunion, and from Alum Cave Trail. In fact, they are better than awesome. It was on one of these Le Conte Trips that we switched from *awesome* to *orgasmic* as our preferred adjective to describe them, partly because boys will be boys and partly because it makes the point that needs to be made, much like an exclamation point at the end of a sentence. Our only other option would have been to resort to profanity!

Just so you won't get the wrong impression, we also discussed a lot of politics and theology. We were still trying to figure out why the world was so screwed up and where we stood in it. Thirty-five years later, I'm still wrestling with many of the same questions. I'd like to get mystical here and say that a week in the Smokies will clear your head and help you to understand reality and your place in the universe. Unfortunately, that never quite happened to me. My time in the Smokies has been a mixture of fatigue, relaxation, meditation, and education. It's been fine fellowship with some good friends. In some sense, it is always a spiritual time, and I have had some epiphanies, but nature hasn't given me the answers to life's great questions. Maybe that's all you can expect from the Smokies, but for me that's enough.

A quick look at a map of the Smokies shows that the park is best visualized as an oval stretching horizontally, east and west. The crest of the Great Smokies runs across the oval from east to west, dividing the park in half. Conveniently, this is also the state line between Tennessee and North Carolina and the route of the famed Appalachian Trail. US 441 (aka Newfound Gap Road) splits the park down the middle from north to south.

Thus, the park is comprised of four quarters. Once you think of the park in those terms, you can begin to place various landmarks in their proper quadrant: Cades Cove is in the northwest; most of the Cherokee Indian Reservation is in the southeast; Mount Le Conte and Mount Cammerer are in the northeast; Forney Creek is in the southwest; Newfound Gap is the four corners point where the quadrants converge.

As an extra step of familiarity, you can learn the names of the dominant side ridges. Visualize the main crest (state line) as the backbone. The side ridges are ribs that extend in roughly perpendicular fashion from the backbone to the outer edges of the oval. These side ridges are not nicely symmetrical and neat, but learning the locations of, say, Jenkins Ridge, Welch Ridge, and Forney Ridge in the southwest quadrant or the Boulevard and Pinnacle Lead in the northeast, is one way to deepen your familiarity with the park.

Between all those side ridges running to the edges of the oval are *rivers* running to the edge of the oval. The ridges are good and wonderful in their own right. Hike them for the same reason George Mallory climbed Everest – because they are there. However, given my attachment to rivers and the trout that live in them, I tend to think of ridges as the places where rivers begin. We call them watersheds – big, rough, steep-sided, tree-and-dirt-and-rock-covered bowls that have hundreds of springs trickling out of them.

It is these small springs that provide your drinking water on a trip into the backcountry, and if the experts are correct, it's contaminated with animal fecal material or a dozen other nasty things. Using words like "pristine" or "pure" when we talk about wilderness is fine if you are a poet or a PR guy for a local chamber of commerce, but even poets are savvy enough to purify their creek water before they drink, just in case the water isn't as pristine as their poetry suggests. The PR guys... well, they probably don't set foot in their pristine wilderness often enough to know.

I don't know if the creek water today is really more contaminated than 100 years ago or if we are just more aware of it today. I once heard Popcorn Sutton, the famous moonshiner, say about the water in a small creek where he was building a still, "There ain't nothing in this water but bear shit." While I'd consider that creek water to be contaminated, his point was that the water was clean, clear, mountain water. Like a lot of other things, contamination is in the eye of the beholder.

Or maybe we're less conditioned to it today, like an American drinking the water in Mexico and suffering the consequences because our soft, civilized tummies aren't up to Montezuma's revenge. Wherever the truth lies, whether you go to Mexico or the Smokies it's best to err on the side of safety and purify all your water.

Back in my younger days you could buy water purification tablets, but in an effort to save money my friends and I would bring a tiny bottle of bleach and put in a few drops per gallon of water. It seemed to work for us; although, the taste was too… *urban*, I guess. Harvey Broome wrote in 1944 that in the old days, many a mountain family moved away to jobs in the city, only to return to the mountains because they couldn't bear the taste of city water. Now I use a purification pump so the water will taste more like trees and rocks and less like chlorine and pavement.

Those trickles converge and grow into the creeks that flow out of the highlands with conviction. They don't meander like lowland rivers that can't decide where they want to go. Rather, mountain rivers flow brashly down narrow valleys, zigzagging only when absolutely necessary. They know where they need to go, and they go, out of the mountains to the Gulf of Mexico. Yes, the Gulf of Mexico. The western continental divide in the Rockies gets all the attention, but there's an eastern continental divide, too, and the Smokies are on the western side of it.

Surely most families who travel across the Rockies stop so the kids can spit or pee down opposite sides of the continental divide. If you travel to the Smokies with your kids, you can't do that. You must get on the Blue Ridge Parkway near the town of Cherokee and drive about an hour east, past Brevard, NC, because the eastern continental divide is a few dozen miles to the east and south of the Smokies. It follows the route of the Blue Ridge Parkway from Virginia south to Asheville and continues south to the South Carolina-Georgia state line. The Blue Ridge Parkway makes a sharp northwest turn near Brevard to leave this eastern divide and enter the Smokies. The rivers to the east of this Blue Ridge divide flow directly into the Atlantic. The rivers to the west of the eastern continental divide ultimately flow west into the Mississippi River, and then the Gulf.

For the lover of rivers, the Smokies are a paradise. There are lots of rivers, and they flow out of the park in several different places around the edges. Starting at Gatlinburg in the north and going clockwise around the park, we find: the West Prong of the Little Pigeon, the Middle Prong of the Little Pigeon, Cosby Creek, Big Creek; Cataloochee Creek, Raven Fork, Oconaluftee River, Deep Creek, Noland Creek, Forney Creek, Hazel Creek, Eagle Creek, Twentymile Creek, Abrams Creek, and Little River. Because these rivers flow out to the edge of the park and beyond, you can drive to most of them using the roads that surround the park. Many of these rivers have nice, easy trails running along them, and you don't have to walk very far to get a sense of being deep in the woods.

As you walk in these mountains and see the large trees and deep forests, it's easy to misunderstand what you are seeing. It feels like deep wilderness that has stood untouched since the beginning of time. It's not. Not even close.

The park has an interesting human history. Of course, the Cherokee Indians roamed these hills, but for the most part they did not live in the depths of the mountains. They tended to live in small farming communities by rivers, such as the Little Tennessee and the Tuckasegee, in the lower elevations around the edges of today's national park. These mountains were primarily their sacred hunting grounds, partly because they were big and majestic but also because they were too rugged and shady for agricultural communities to flourish.

The phrase "river of life" is not just a figure of speech used in hymns and poems. It's also a literal description. Not only does the human body need a steady supply of water, human communities thrive on it as well. All the cradles of civilization from Egypt and Babylon to Knoxville and Asheville to Gatlinburg and Oconaluftee were rivers. The town where you live is located where it is because that's where the water is.

(Exceptions to this rule, such as Las Vegas, will have their day of reckoning with Mother Nature in the next few years, and the fight for the last few drops of water will surely get ugly.) This connection between water and life is seen at even the smallest level in the Smokies. Find the rock foundations of a cabin or the remnants of an old CCC camp, and you'll find a creek or spring nearby.

Significant human impact upon these mountains began in the early to mid 1800s as white pioneers, mostly Scots-Irish, moved in from the north and east. I've been told by people who should know that Scots or Scottish refers to people from Scotland, whereas Scotch is the whiskey. Apparently, that's the way the experts talk (although, the Scotch Tape people haven't bought into that terminology yet). So, a guy with a Scottish accent sounds like Sean Connery. A guy with a Scotch accent sounds like he's drunk.

By the late 1800s there were small communities with strong Scots-Irish roots scattered throughout the Smokies. These mountaineers were primarily small-scale, subsistence farmers, living in small log cabins. These are the people Horace Kephart described in *Our Southern Highlanders* in 1913, many of whom were stereotypical mountain hillbillies. In the late 1800s and early 1900s the logging companies began accumulating huge tracts of land and setting up their operations. Small camps and towns grew up around these logging operations. Log cabins became passé in favor of finished lumber houses. By the 1920s and 30s, there were also several exclusive hunting and fishing clubs and several hotels and resort communities within today's boundaries of the park.

All these groups – the Cherokee and mountaineers, the logging companies and resorts – were drawn to the rivers for the water and water power, as well as ease of access and recreation. These rivers and watersheds were the location of a great deal of human activity, and it was ultimately the destructive nature of this activity that led to calls for the government to step in and save the mountains by creating a national park. The good news, from a conservationist's perspective, is that the logging was stopped, and the companies sold their land and went elsewhere. The sad news is that the simple families who had lived here were forced to leave as well. On balance, I'm glad it happened. The Smokies were saved for people like me, and you. We couldn't enjoy them otherwise, but our joy and pleasure came at a price to the people who lived here.

Quite honestly, many residents were happy that someone was interested in buying their land at a decent price. After all, their land was rugged and pretty, but in the 1930s, "rugged and pretty" couldn't put food on the table. These folks took the money and left, amazed that anyone would actually pay for such steep, rocky soil. A few long-time residents who were deeply rooted on their land got lawyers and fought the law and the law won, as it usually does. It's probably no coincidence that those families who had been here the longest also had the best land because it's the best land that gets settled first. They were the ones most reluctant to leave. Some arranged life-long leases allowing them to stay on the land until their death. I bought home-grown honey from Kermit Caughron a long-time resident of Cades Cove well into the 1980s. I didn't have the presence of mind to talk to him about the old days because I was younger then and thought I'd live forever, and I guess I assumed he would, too. When he died in 1999, it was like a library of local history had burned to the ground. And the NPS finally got his land free and clear, but only over his dead body. Literally.

Consequently, a walk along any river in the park will, if you look closely, still show signs of the human activity of the pre-park days. I occasionally fish the Middle Prong of the Little River in the Tremont area, near Townsend. As I wade up the river, I occasionally have to side-step a piece of steel railroad track sticking out of the bank, a remnant of the logging company train tracks from a century ago. The same railroad remnants can be found in most of the rivers that flow out of the park. In fact, the riverside trail you hike on was either an old wagon road or a railroad bed.

This also means that the trees you see on most of your river hikes are "second-growth" forests. The individual trees and the forest as a whole are less than 100 years old, which is young in wilderness forest terms. Thankfully, the forest looks a lot like it would have 1,000 years ago – a deep, green forest composed of a huge variety of deciduous trees with a few conifers and lots of rhododendron thrown in – but virgin forest is not exactly what you are witnessing on most of your Smoky Mountain hikes. Of course, if you are knowledgeable of the flora of these mountains then you know about things like the chestnut blight that wiped out the chestnut trees and the CCC that replanted thousands of trees, so you'd be technically correct in saying that the forest does *not* look *exactly* like it did 1,000 years ago.

So maybe the best description of the forest is that it *feels* like it did 1,000 years ago – deep, green, cool, and moist – thus avoiding the debates about blights, exotic species, reforestation, and climax forests. Walk into the forest, close your eyes, breathe deep, listen. This is how it felt centuries ago.

My wife, Phyllis, and I have walked the Porters Creek Trail in the Greenbrier area of the park many times. This trail is heavily traveled in April and May because of the extravagant wildflower display that this trail is famous for. On a recent fall hike our attention was diverted away from the flowers (because of the season of the year) and toward the trail and hillside. As we walked we saw old rock walls, crumbling chimneys, spring houses, and a graveyard. There was even an old 1930s hiking club cabin with pull-down bunks and kitchen partially intact. We were pleased to see that there were only a few names scratched on the walls. Fortunately, people who enjoy defacing historic sites tend to be lazy, so after you get more than a mile from the parking lot, the graffiti on these old buildings diminishes significantly.

We spent a pleasant afternoon just moseying around the walls and chimneys, trying to figure out the floor plan of the cabin, or guessing where the daffodils will sprout in the spring, or reading tombstones trying to recreate the story of the generations who had lived and died here.

There's a lingering sorrow in the cemeteries that are scattered around the park. In the small cemetery one mile up Porters Creek Trail one of the first grave stones you'll encounter provides a stark reminder of the harshness of life without advanced medicine. It simply says: Mary Whaley, Born & Died, Aug 11, 1909. Far too many grave stones in rural communities of the early 1900s have a single date etched on their surface, accompanied by that hauntingly familiar phrase: "Born & Died." The Smokies were no exception and because of their ruggedness, may have been harsher than most.

The grave stones of every cemetery are squares of a quilt that tells the story of an interwoven community in which the life and death of each member touched the hearts and lives of nearly everyone else in the cove. That closeness and connectedness which we associate with small, rural communities also created vulnerability. The death of a neighbor left a void in the lives of those who remained, just as tearing a square from a quilt not only leaves a hole but also diminishes the loveliness of the pattern. Every Smokies cemetery tells a sad story. *Many* sad stories.

A neat thing about these historic remnants is that they are usually surprises, so you feel like you've really discovered something. I'm sure that in a filing cabinet or computer somewhere at park headquarters there's an inventory of all the crumbling, pre-park structures, but this information doesn't make it into the visitor guides and general park information, so when you walk on a trail you usually have little or no idea what crumbling remnants you'll find. Maybe any chimney you touch or tombstone inscription you read has already been touched or read by thousands of visitors before you. On the other hand, you have taken the initiative to get off the main road to a quiet corner of the park, so you might be one of just a few dozen people who have seen and touched these things in the past 80 years. Either way, the "What's this doing here?" factor provides a sense of satisfaction that eating 37 cockroaches just can't match because the point is not to be the first or the only person to do something; the point is to do something worthwhile, even if you aren't the only one to do it.

All of us have some sort of paradigm – a body of knowledge and interests that enables us to notice and understand certain details in the world around us – which often shows up as an obsession. Several years ago, as my wife and I were wrapped up in building our house, I'd ponder the siding or porch or landscaping of every house that I'd drive by. Our house became an entity that demanded not only our time and money, but also our minds and souls. We'd wake up in the morning thinking about what needed to be done, and we'd go to bed at night thinking about what hadn't been done. It became the focus of our lives and our reason for existence, which is why I began calling it the Golden Calf. Everything we did was judged by whether it would serve as an appropriate sacrifice to the Golden Calf. Would green shutters be a proper adornment on the GC? Would the GC prefer azaleas or rose bushes? Will the GC bless us if we use red brick? I didn't hike or fish much that year. The Golden Calf forbade it because you can't serve two masters.

Back in my younger days while I was still in college and a rabid backpacker, I knew the location of all the most popular hiking trails in the Southern Appalachians and many of the lesser known trails as well. I lived in a world of lofty ridges and panoramic views. Every map's purpose was to lead me to mountain trails. Every trail's end was a mountain top with a view. The rivers were merely an afterthought. That was my topographical paradigm.

I still love those high places and I walk to them often – I've sat on the top of Mount Le Conte half a dozen times in the past year and Mount Cammerer twice as often – but as I've aged I've exchanged brute force for finesse as I've shifted to fly fishing and day hiking as my primary outdoor passions. So backpacking has become a means to an end; it's my mode of transportation to good trout water on mountain streams or isolated day hikes in the backcountry. Since I also kayak and canoe to good fishing and hiking spots, the variety of my outdoor activities has actually *increased*, which, from what I've observed, is unusual for a guy whose prime years are a shrinking speck in the rear view mirror.

This shift in passions has led to a shift in paradigms. I've lost touch with some of the trails and peaks of the southern Appalachians. I can't recall off the top of my head whether Wesser Bald is north or south of the Nantahala Outdoor Center. Or, what are the names of the campsite and trail to the top of Mount Mitchell? Where do you park to hike to Standing Indian? I used to know. I can find these places quickly on a map, I know exactly where to look, but I would have to look.

Now I am more in touch with the rivers and manways in this east Tennessee and western North Carolina region. Ask me the location of the Little River, Oconaluftee River, Clinch River, Hiwassee River, or Slickrock Creek, and I can tell you where they are, how to get there, and where and how to fish them. Well, actually, I'll tell you *if* you are a catch and release fisherman. If you fish with salmon eggs and treble hooks and keep your fish, then I'll tell you I've only *heard* of the Little River, but I think it's someplace in Mississippi, and if you'll start now you can be in Tupelo by tomorrow afternoon. This bit of deceit is necessary to prevent too many folks from fishing in my rivers and catching my fish because these rivers can get emptied out pretty quickly. And, yes, I'm aware that I called them *my* rivers and fish.

One unique feature of fly fishing in the Smokies is that you'll spend some time hiking *by* rivers but much more time hiking *in* them. Because you keep moving and spend only a few minutes in each pool or sluice, fishing in a Smokies river amounts to a wet, slow, sloppy hike. You are in the river, knee to chest deep, in the middle, wading against the current, hopping on and over rocks, ducking under fallen trees and rhododendron branches. And, importantly, you'll have a fly rod in your hand.

Searching for fish while carrying a fly rod makes you a predator, which creates a connection between you and your surroundings that normally doesn't exist. You are not just looking at a pretty river. You are not merely *in* the river. You are *involved* with the river. You become a part of it. It's what the ancient Greeks called *koinonia* and we call *communion*. At that moment you belong in the river just as surely as the water, rocks, and fish. You are, for the moment, inhabiting the same environmental niche as an otter, which may not sound very impressive, but every now and then it's just good to be a wild animal of any sort.

Norman Maclean's book, *A River Runs Through It*, is a story about life, family, and fly fishing on a trout river in Montana. The book tells about Norm and his brother and the river that gave them memories and held them together. Its opening sentence is a classic in fly fishing literature: "In our family, there was no clear line between religion and fly fishing."

Most of us, myself included, can vividly describe the moment of our "conversion" to fly fishing as if it happened just yesterday. In fact, some true believers would summon the Grand Inquisitor to investigate my use of quote marks around *conversion.* "Do you mean to imply, Mr. Hoover, that a fly fishing conversion is not an actual religious conversion?" Such heresy is not taken lightly among The Enlightened of the Priory of Fly Fishing.

But it is the last line in Maclean's book that speaks most poignantly to me because it speaks of memories and communion, and of the outdoor paradigm I've adopted as I've grown older: "I am haunted by waters." If I ever write the great, 21st century, American novel, that will be my opening line. It will be the story of a brave but weary hero (me, of course) who triumphs over personal tragedy, societal apathy, and the Illuminati to save the world from war, racism, and environmental catastrophe. Yes, mountains, rivers, and trout will somehow be in there, too. Somehow.

Everyone is haunted by something: a misspent youth, bad credit, a busy schedule, a career, a house under construction. Considering the alternatives, being haunted by a love of the outdoors – by the *need* to be outdoors – seems a healthy alternative. Being haunted by street names, houses, stores, electronics, sidewalks, and offices but not by rivers or ridges comes dangerously close to missing the point, the sign of a misspent adulthood. If your friends can name the nearest night club but not the nearest trail that can be hiked or river that can be fished, then it's time to re-examine your peer group and to shift your paradigm. There are probably support groups available; you know, to help you overcome your illness. Or, just go to the mountains and take a long walk by a noisy, tumbling river. That paradigm shift that you desperately need is more likely to happen there, on that trail by that river, than in the city because the road to recovery isn't a road. It's a trail. In the mountains.

Chapter 4
Hazel Creek

My old, white, fiberglass canoe is nothing to brag about; in fact, it's something to be embarrassed by, but it gets the job done. It's flat bottomed, but without a keel, so it's supposed to work on both moving water and flat water, which really means it's not ideal for either. It's a jack of all trades and master of none, much like my 8½ foot, five weight fly rod. It's too much if you want to fish a small, limber rod, and it's not enough if you need a big, powerful rod.

This canoe has been on family vacations to Cape Cod and the ponds of Acadia National Park, as well as local day trips on Cherokee Lake, Big South Fork River, and the French Broad River. It's been on fishing trips to the Clinch, Hiwassee, Watauga, and South Holston Rivers. It sometimes goes with me to the AuSable River in Michigan for a week in June. It is plain white, but the bottom and sides have drips of brown deck stain from the time I stained my back deck and was too lazy to cover up the canoe that was hanging below. It also has some black globs of epoxy on the front and back ends where the fiberglass has been splintered by river rocks. The canoe rack on the back of my truck is homemade out of 2 x 6s, so when we put the white, brown, and black canoe on the homemade wooden rack, you don't have to look at the license plate to know that we are from the hills of east Tennessee. We drive down I-40, reinforcing the stereotypes held by every out of state driver who passes us. The only thing missing is some silver duct tape on the canoe and Granny on top in her rocking chair. Well, Ellie Mae is missing, too, but she's not invited because she's a girl. (That, and the fact that she wouldn't return our calls.)

One of my fishing partners, Greg Harrell, and I had wanted to explore Fontana Lake for several years, and we somehow finally managed to synchronize our summer schedules to make the Fontana trip happen; although, we didn't call it that. We called it the Hazel Creek Trip, because that's where we were going to camp and fish. So, we set a date and then told our other fishing partners, Tim Landefeld and Keith Oakes, about it. If four of us went, we'd take two canoes. If three, then a canoe and a kayak. If two, just a canoe.

Tim, Keith, Greg, and I fish often together, but not often enough. We live in the same town, go to the same church, our families are all connected, and we all fly fish for trout. Tim is the one most likely to fly fish for bluegill and bass because his wife's family has a farm with several ponds an hour north of here. The rest of us aren't opposed to fishing for bass and bluegill, but we don't ever seem to get around to actually doing it. I wouldn't call us trout snobs, just guys with limited time and a clearly defined set of fishing priorities.

So the plan was to paddle across the lake to the mouth of Hazel Creek, where it flows out of the southwest edge of the Great Smoky Mountains National Park and into Fontana Lake. For reasons that I'm sure they regret, Tim and Keith couldn't make it, so it was just the two Gregs in my canoe.

There were several reasons why we paddled. First of all, you can hike to Hazel Creek, but it would take a couple of days, and it would be very, very tough. Now, of course, we want to be seen as two very, very tough guys, right? But here's where the second factor kicks in. Paddling to a Smokies campsite is something we'd never done before, and we thought it would add an interesting, missing ingredient to a trip. (Which it did.) We also pride ourselves on pulling our own weight, being masculinely self-sufficient, and there's nothing more self-sufficient than loading camping equipment into a canoe and heading out into the water and woods for a few days.

The only flaw in the plan was that the marina near Fontana Dam where we thought we'd put in was over 5 miles from the mouth of Hazel. If the marina wanted to charge us $10 or $20 dollars for the privilege of using their facilities, we would try to find a parking lot at the dam and carry the canoe down to the waterside; but that would add yet another mile or two to the paddle. We weren't sure how fast we could paddle up the lake, but we didn't want to spend most of the day paddling. We thought the canoe part of the trip would be fun, but it was a *fishing* trip after all. We wanted to get to Hazel Creek and *fish*.

Fortunately my wife, Phyllis, and I were in the Bryson City area in early June. We scouted around and found a decent, national forest boat ramp right across the lake from the inlet of Hazel Creek. This cut the paddle down to 3 miles, so even if we paddled at one mile an hour, we'd only be on the water for three hours. That seemed about right.

As it turned out, we paddled at a rate of about 3 mph and spent only one hour paddling. We were in a bit of a hurry, since we didn't really know how fast we were going or exactly where the mouth of the river was. Well, we knew where the mouth was on the map, and we knew we were heading straight for it, but the conjunction of water and tree covered ridges makes it very difficult to judge distances and angles. Several times we thought we were approaching the end of the water, only to discover that it was just a bend in the channel. The apprehension pushed us to hurry a bit more than we should have.

There was also some peer pressure at work. You might think of two guys in a canoe as a cooperative endeavor, and I suppose that's how it looks from a distance, but we're talking about two *guys*, each with a paddle, and each having several decades-worth of male ego infused within him. So a three mile paddle comes to look less like a team sport and more like a boxing match. We each paddled hard, not necessarily trying to outdo the other, but definitely trying not to be *outdone by* the other, which in the end amounts to the same thing.

Since it was my canoe, I sat in the back. Now in a canoe, you don't exactly *steer*, but it is the job of the guy in the back to make sure you follow a straight line. If you are both paddling on opposite sides, then you'll go straight, unless one of you is paddling harder or stronger than the other, in which case you begin to bear to the right or left, depending on who is winning the paddling duel. Greg is left handed, so he usually paddled on the right, and I being right handed usually paddled on the left, so we were both paddling to our strengths. Several times during the paddle I'd feel the canoe bear to the left as Greg was out-paddling me. In such a situation I had only three options: tell him to stop paddling for a second (a clear sign of weakness on my part); stick my paddle in the water like a rudder and actually steer us back to a straight line (which is noisy and sloppy and, therefore, can't be done covertly); or, I could paddle harder (which is painful but enables me to save face). I usually tried option three, with an occasional "let's rest to enjoy the scenery," which we both knew was an admission of defeat. So, we made pretty good time.

If you'll look at a map of the Smokies you can see how the lake and the landscape intertwine. Fontana Lake was created by damming up the Little Tennessee River in 1944. As the water rose it moved not only up but also across the valley and into the side valleys of the rivers that flowed into the Little Tennessee. Eagle Creek, Hazel Creek, Forney Creek, and Noland Creek all still flow south out of the park, but they now flow into a high, deep, wide lake rather than a low, shallow, narrow river. The lake has flooded what used to be the last mile or two of these south-flowing creeks. You can call them *channels* or the Norwegian term *fjords*. Either way, as you paddle up toward the mouth of the creek there is 50 or 100 feet of water below you. And the bottom of the lake at that point is covered with rotting logs, the old creek bed, a road, and a few rock chimneys and walls – the remnants of the old creek valley and the forest and people that lived there.

One result was that numerous towns, roads, and farms that had sprung up along the Little Tennessee River and its tributaries were drowned. That was one of the most perplexing aspects of building these TVA dams in the 1940s. I live near Cherokee Lake which has a similar story. When I look out my back window I see a lake and islands, but what I'm really seeing is a flooded river and hilltops. Every fall TVA lowers the lake levels so more islands (hilltops) become exposed. I paddled out to a small island in the middle of the lake behind our house a few Octobers ago. It's barely covered when the lake is full in the summer and becomes visible in the fall and winter. I discovered that all the rocks that I'd been seeing on it were not natural, eroded rocks. They were blocks and tile and foundation stones from an old house. I don't know who owned it, but they had a great view from their hilltop home of the confluence of Mossy Creek and the Holston River. Although today the hills surrounding Cherokee Lake are mostly wooded, this island top shows no signs of trees. I suspect that in the 1930s and 40s this hill and the river valleys were cleared farm and pasture land, before Cherokee Dam and Lake. It was a classic case of individual rights vs. community benefits. The government took (and paid for) the land to create a dam and lake by which they could generate hydroelectricity that would benefit thousands of people. It has worked out well, but not without some pain for a few.

Fontana has a similar tale, with the added twist that the land immediately north of the new lake – the Eagle Creek and Hazel Creek watersheds – was *not* part of the original Great Smoky Mountains National Park. When Fontana Lake filled up in 1944, the farms and communities on the lake's north shore were now cut off from the south shore. What had formerly been a simple river crossing over a modest bridge would now require a lake crossing by boat or a long commute around the lake. And so the people who had lived in this sliver of land, with the lake to their south and the new national park to their north, were forced to sell their land and move. Their land was added to the park, whose boundaries finally stretched all the way to the new Fontana Lake.

It is the remnants of those old communities that you can still see when you visit Hazel Creek. These communities, farms, cabins, and cemeteries were not flooded; they were isolated and finally annexed by the park. Today, this isolation factor is one of the alluring qualities of the southwest quadrant of the park. Whereas Fontana Lake once cut the north shore folks off from the rest of the world, it now works in just the opposite direction. All of us have been cut off from the north shore valleys and ridges. They are difficult to get to. You'll either have to hike for a day or two, paddle for an hour or two, pay to be ferried across the lake, or use your own boat.

Greg and I paddled across and dragged our canoe into the weeds next to the mouth of the river. There's some trepidation in doing this because the backcountry campsite is a 10 minute walk further up the trail, so unless you want to drag your canoe all that way, you'll be stowing it by the mouth of Hazel Creek. I don't normally worry much about my gear being stolen on these backcountry trips because the people you encounter aren't the thieving type. However, it has also occurred to me that a guy with a motor boat and a rope could make some money by motoring up to the mouths of Hazel, Eagle, and Forney Creeks and stealing canoes and kayaks. Or, someone might get a kick out of hiking or paddling in, camping for a day or two, and then engaging in some minor vandalism, such as trashing a canoe. These possibilities didn't keep me awake for the two nights we were there, but this is 21st century America, and a few people will do mindless acts of harm just to break the monotony of a self-absorbed existence. But, like I said, those types don't usually show up at backcountry campsites in our national parks. So, we split the difference. We didn't go to extra lengths to hide the canoe, but we did hide the *paddles* extremely well, hoping that anyone trying to steal a canoe probably wouldn't think to bring a paddle, and wouldn't be clever enough to find a well-hidden one.

Happily, when we came back to the canoe a couple of days later, things were exactly as we had left them, including the well-hidden paddles... which I wasn't clever enough to find. After letting me wander and wonder long enough to become convinced that some confused soul had actually left the canoe but stolen the paddles, Greg walked over to the weed bed where we had stashed the paddles and pulled them out. Obviously, the same elves that hide my wallet and keys at home every night had followed me all the way to Hazel Creek to hide my paddles. You would think they'd have better things to do.

The campsite where we spent our two nights was called Proctor, named after the town that used to be at that spot. The campsite was large (by backcountry standards) and well-used but not abused. However, one thing did surprise me. Proctor is the one place in the Smokies where conflicting camping paradigms bump into each other on a regular basis.

Normally, at backcountry sites if you see anyone else they are usually young backpackers – long haired, unshaven, Sierra Club types who recycle and have pro-green stickers on the bumpers of their fuel efficient cars. Their tents are small and light – made for carrying on a backpack. Their equipment is sparse – small stoves, a few clothes, no luxuries. This is how

Greg and I had packed, as we would for a typical backpacking trip, plus our fishing gear. But we were surprised to see several camp setups that looked like something you'd see in a developed campground like Elkmont or Cades Cove. These sites would have a tent too large to carry on a backpack and double-burner Coleman stoves for cooking their elaborate eggs and bacon breakfasts. They would also have a cooler full of ice and cold drinks. I hadn't expected that, but once I got there and saw it, I understood. Many people who spend the night in the Proctor campsite get there by their own boat or the ferry. They can bring a lot of heavy stuff that a couple of guys with backpacks in a canoe wouldn't even think of bringing. Once off the boat they transport their tents, stoves, and coolers with carts that are a cross between a shopping cart and a wheelbarrow, but with large wheels for rolling over dirt and rocks.

Some folks get to Proctor and then realize that they forgot to bring ice or bacon or whatever, so they "run to the store" to buy what they need. The guy who told me this story is a spartan, backpacker who was absolutely mystified by the concept of running to the store in the middle of a backcountry camping trip, so he asked the guy what he meant because he was sure he had misunderstood. The guy explained that he would hop in his bass boat, jet to Fontana Village near the dam, and be back in about an hour with the missing bag of nachos. To each his own, I suppose, but I've always considered preparation and risk to be important components of a camping trip. You live by the old Boy Scout motto of always being prepared, and if that fails then you make do with what you have. In bass boat camping your biggest risk is losing your boat keys, "being prepared" means having enough gas for a trip to the marina, and "make do" means absolutely nothing at all. Somehow, I don't think that's what the Boy Scouts had in mind.

Proctor was fine once we had re-oriented our expectations, but next time we'll escape the onslaught of ice chests, iron skillets, and stereos by doing what bears, mountain lions, and Boy Scouts have been doing for decades – we'll retreat deeper into the wilderness, to the Sugar Fork or Bone Valley campsite, even though it will mean an extra 5 or 6 mile hike, one way.

In addition to the different clientele, the Proctor site itself was different from the typical backcountry site. It was larger, plus there was even an old house with a small pasture and a couple of horses just across the creek from the campsite. The house was left over from the pre-park days, but I don't know what the horses were doing there. The park rangers probably use the house as a bunk house and the horses as transportation into the backcountry. There was also an old, deteriorating bus behind the house. It was old, but it wasn't 1940's vintage so it wasn't a relic of the pre-park days. The former residents and descendants of the Proctor families were guaranteed (as part of the agreement to sell their land) access to the abandoned, family cemeteries in the park. The bus was probably an old vehicle that was used several times a year to transport groups of former residents and their families further up the creek valley to these tiny, family burial grounds. As we fished and explored over the next couple of days, we ran across a small cemetery about 6 miles further up the creek. We could tell from the plastic flowers, trinkets, and general maintenance that it was still being kept up and visited. The trail up Hazel Creek is not exactly a gravel road by today's standards, but it's wide enough to formerly have been a railroad bed and a narrow road for wagons and, in the 1930s and 40s, for cars and trucks. I've been told that ATVs, small pickup trucks, and SUVs are ferried across the lake and are now being used instead of the bus.

When I first learned of it, this human history of the Smokies disappointed me. I wanted the Smokies to be a vast, untouched wilderness that only a few leather moccasins had trod. My illusion of the Smokies included only native flora and fauna, there being no place for roads, railroads, logging, corn fields, towns, hunting clubs, hotels, and resort communities. But eventually I came to realize that I live east of the Mississippi, and if I wanted unblemished wilderness I'd have to move to the heart of the Everglades. Since I like history and sociology, the progression of human life in this region from native hunter-gatherers and horticulturalists, to pioneers, to loggers, to visitors like me is fascinatingly imperfect and real. It is what it is, and if you want to become familiar with these mountains, you might as well embrace not only the natural side but the human side, too.

That's one reason that I love the Hazel Creek valley. It is typical Smoky Mountain beauty, mixed with still-visible remnants of human history, and most of that human history is not the history of wars, battles, kings, and politicians; it is the history of common, hard working families – growing corn, raising a few cows and chickens, loving family, helping neighbors, hiding their stills from the tax man, going to church, and cutting down the trees and eroding the soil that makes this place beautiful because, in spite of what we'd like to think, they didn't have the riches and comfort to enable them to see past their need to grow food and make a living. How could people come to a place so beautiful and despoil it? Well, the beauty and quiet were nice, but that's a luxury that not everyone can afford to notice or to make a priority. They came here because they could, because the land was available, and they needed land. As long as there were only a few of them, their impact was minimal, but the Industrial Revolution gave them the tools and access to extract more products from the land (timber, copper, food, fish), and that's what they did.

It's one of the ironies of modern life that our consumption-driven, resource-depleting lifestyles have provided us with an unprecedented degree of ease and comfort, and it is this comfortable lifestyle that frees us from the daily battle to obtain food and shelter and enables us to appreciate wilderness as something to be loved rather than to be conquered. If a society is lucky it will rise to that level of understanding and appreciation before it has actually destroyed all the beautiful wilderness in the process.

A lot of wilderness was preserved in the western US not only because there was so much of it left unmolested by the late 1800s, but also because the eastern US had developed into a softer, wealthier, more "civilized" region that was now able to appreciate the wild beauty of the natural world. Yes, most of the rapacious captains of industry were in the east, but their wealth helped to create an elevated vision of the great outdoors as something beautiful, something worth preserving rather than exploiting. (The Rockefellers are the perfect example of this, helping to save the Smokies and numerous other national parks.)

Luckily, there were still a few places that could be preserved – mostly out west, but one or two patches here in the east, too.

The Smoky Mountains just barely snuck in under the wire. They had been inhabited and used, almost used up, by the logging companies, but they were still rugged and lightly inhabited enough for people to see the potential in them, to see what they once were and could perhaps be again. Thus the Smokies were saved in the 1930s, not as a vast, untouched wilderness, but more like a reclamation project. It is for that reason that about two-thirds of the forests in the Smokies are second-growth forests. The Smokies in general, and Hazel Creek in particular, are not an example of nature unspoiled, but they are an example of nature reclaiming what is hers, and it appears that the operation was a success. The patient is well on the way to making a full recovery.

This land belonged to the Cherokee people, but a series of treaties during the late 1700s and early 1800s gradually displaced them, the final blows being the Indian Removal Act passed by Congress in 1830 and the Treaty of New Echota in 1835. Those two pieces of legislation are the reason why there are more Cherokees in Oklahoma than in the southern Appalachians, even though the only Cherokee reservation is the one here in the Smokies. After the final removal via the infamous Trail of Tears in 1838-9, the government sold the land to railroads, businessmen, land speculators, and private families. By 1900, there were scattered family farms and small settlements in this southwest portion of the Smokies, but by 1910 most of this land had been purchased or leased by logging companies: Ritter in the Hazel Creek valley, Montvale in Eagle Creek, Norwood in Forney Creek, and Champion in the Deep Creek and Oconaluftee watersheds.

These companies employed men to build roads, lay railroad tracks, cut the trees, and saw the timber. Many of these workers were local men who still owned their own land mingled between the logging companies' holdings. Some of these men actually sold their land to the logging companies but were allowed to continue living and farming the land, what amounted to selling the timber but keeping the land. This agreement could work out well for a man who wanted more land cleared to grow more crops or pasture more cattle. Some of the loggers were men from the surrounding regions who moved in and lived in cabins or barracks in the small logging towns that were springing up next to these Smokies rivers. Most of today's developed campgrounds, ranger stations, and visitor centers were once the sites of these logging towns: Smokemont on the Oconaluftee, Elkmont on the Little River, Fontana on the Little Tennessee, Crestmont on Big Creek, and Proctor on Hazel Creek. Of course, these towns created the opportunity for local farmers to sell their excess food and moonshine to the loggers. The mountain families of the Smokies were being drawn in to the larger cash economy of the US, which is always a mixed blessing.

So, we camped at Proctor in the deep shade of the poplars and maples, with an occasional white pine that hadn't yet surrendered to the growing hardwood forest. (Scattered pines in a hardwood forest are usually a sign of prior human activity.) This heavily forested site was once the site of the Proctor school's ball field and swimming hole, and the fact that you really have to stretch your imagination to visualize a school and ball field is merely a testament to the power of nature to reclaim her own. It's the same process at work that makes that tuft of grass grow up through the crack in your sidewalk or weeds sneak into your flowerbed. In the Smokies it's just on a much larger scale.

A trail guide called *Hiking Trails of the Smokies* is a great little book of details, both natural and historical, of all the trails in the Smokies. Its description of this Hazel Creek section mentions that Proctor's main street of the early 1940's included a line of maple trees, a wooden sidewalk, and a row of painted houses with picket fences. Again, only those of us with a vivid imagination can picture it. I suppose you could say that Proctor is a ghost town, except there aren't enough buildings left for even the ghosts to inhabit. They left a long time ago.

After setting up our two small tents and throwing our sleeping bags and pads in, we spent a few minutes looking around, and then got down to business. We assembled our fly rods and pulled the line through the eyes. We each checked our leader, making sure the final piece was several feet of 5x or 6x.

A 6x tippet is merely a piece of monofilament fishing line that is very, very thin – 5 thousandths of an inch in diameter. If you use a thicker tippet you risk spooking the fish when you cast your fly. If I use 5x tippet, which is a whopping 1 thousandth of an inch thicker, the fish can sometimes notice the difference. With the larger 5x I'll get splashy, last-second refusals by the fish, but switching to the smaller diameter 6x line sometimes results in more hooked fish. The key word in those sentences being *sometimes*, as in "Sometimes it matters, and sometimes it doesn't."

I started with a size 14 Parachute Adams and Greg started with a size 14 Thunderhead. Although I didn't watch him tie on his fly, I know that's what he used because it's just about the only fly he ever uses in the Smokies. Both of these flies are dry (floating) flies, and the only difference between an Adams and a Thunderhead is that the hackle (rooster feather) of a Thunderhead is brown, while the hackle of an Adams is a mixture of brown and grizzly (mixed gray & white, creating a sort of silver glow). Other than that, same fly. Of course, my Adams was a *Parachute* Adams, so that was a stylistic difference. That means that the hackle of my fly was tied on around the base of the wing on a horizontal plane, rather than the standard style of wrapping the hackle around the "throat" of the fly like a shirt collar.

Things go smoothly when we both use dry flies because in the strange world of fly fishing, dry flies are more righteous than wet (sinking) flies, and fish caught on dry flies are superior to those caught on wet flies. Some dry fly purists will silently subtract an inch or two from the length of any fish that their partner catches with a wet fly; although, it's been my experience that the math of fly fishing isn't that precise. Instead of subtracting inches, most dry fly purists simply value such a fish less, as if his partner had just caught a bluegill instead of a trout, in which case it doesn't even matter how big the fish is. To the purist, a trout is a gentleman and is to be caught by a gentleman using tactics befitting a gentleman, or he will be caught not at all. There are some things up with which the purist shall not put, such as ending a sentence with a preposition, marrying below one's class, and catching a trout with a wet fly.

So when we both fish dry flies, we can give our end-of-the-day fishing report to each other with a clear conscience. A ten inch trout is, free and clear, a full-blooded trout and a full ten inches. However, if I caught a ten inch trout on a weighted, wet fly then Greg would be obligated to refrain from any display of enthusiasm as he nodded in muted approval. He would silently question the size and species of my fish and my veracity because someone who would stoop to fishing a wet fly on Hazel Creek is the kind of person who would also stretch the truth a bit around the edges, or in this case, stretch a trout at both ends.

Neither of us is a dry fly snob because we both will fish subsurface flies when the fish demand it, but it's not something to be proud of, and it's not something you want to be the first to do. There's an unspoken game of chicken here. It's bad enough to switch from a dry fly to a wet fly, but it's even worse if you make the switch before your partner does, and it's worse still if he sees you do it. The guy who gives in first shows that he doesn't have the guts to keep doing the right thing. He's weak and deserves the taunting that he'll receive: "Sheesh! If you're going to start fishing with bait, I guess I might as well, too." Or, simply, "I knew I shouldn't have brought you." Or, if your partner catches the first fish of the day on a wet fly, you simply say, casually and without making eye contact, "So, I guess we're still getting skunked." Touché. Game, set, and match. In your face. And scene.

All this nonsense makes us look like dry fly snobs, but none of us is as committed to the dry fly as it seems. We are, however, committed to working our way up the pecking order by taunting each other at every opportunity. It's the foundation stone of male culture, so if my partner gives in and changes to a wet fly, I am obligated to verbally abuse him – until I quietly sneak away and change to a wet fly, too. Then the taunting will stop… until one of us makes a mistake or shows some hint of human frailty – such as slipping on a wet rock, catching a small fish, losing a big fish, eating a low calorie lunch, having a pastel colored water bottle, wearing cheap socks, tangling your fly line, snagging your fly on a tree branch, using a strike indicator, using a pink strike indicator, using a strike indicator but still catching no fish, using sun screen, catching fish with a cheap fly rod, not catching fish with an expensive fly rod, wearing a clean hat, wearing a work hat rather than a hat used exclusively for fishing, taking a nap.... That's a partial list of the ones with which I am personally acquainted.

One good thing about male subculture: it's refreshingly uncomplicated, just like it was in middle school, although now with a little less cruelty and a little more light-heartedness.

After tying on our dry flies (a rule for the non-purist: at least *start* with a dry fly), we both put on our breathable waders and our wading boots (with felt bottoms to reduce, but not eliminate, slipping on the river rocks) and walked upstream. After a few hundred yards, we split up. I got in and started fishing whereas Greg walked about a hundred yards further upstream, built a small rock cairn on a boulder in the middle of the river, and began fishing upstream.

When I fish the Smokies with Greg, we always split up like this. Greg is a loner in real life and even more so in the mountains. He doesn't want to be crowded when he fishes the Smokies, and merely seeing another person, even a friend, is *crowding* in his dictionary. So we both worked our way upstream, casting to innumerable small chutes and runs, dapping behind rocks, and catching some feisty, little rainbows. Greg even caught a couple of twelve inchers, which are very good fish in the Smokies. (He had a tattered dry fly dangling from the end of his line as a character witness, so I was forced to believe his fishing report.)

When I got to the small rock cairn that Greg had built in the middle of the river, I knew to get out of the water and walk upstream. If I continued to fish, I'd be fishing water that he had just fished. Fly fishing is intended to make the task of catching trout more challenging, a matter of finesse rather than brute force, but most of us will draw the line at fishing in recently-fished water. As a friend of mine once said, "When I go out for a day of fishing, I first have to decide whether I want to *fly* fish or *catch* fish." Those are clearly the words of a guy who hasn't yet given his heart and soul over to fly fishing. Nevertheless, he does have a point: fly fishing isn't a particularly efficient way to catch fish. But I think it's the *best* way to catch fish, if by "best" we mean beautiful, poetic, challenging, or expensive... but it's still nice to catch a fish every now and then.

We continued in this leap frog fashion for several hours, sometimes seeing each other and stopping to share fishing reports. I don't recall much in the way of insect activity, so it was typical Smokies fishing, casting to good-looking water rather than casting to feeding fish. By late afternoon I was ready for a nap, so I walked back to Proctor, and slept in my tent, thus preserving my reputation as a lazy fisherman. Greg kept fishing. He's had work and family issues that have kept him from fishing much during the last few years, so he makes the most of it when a fishing opportunity presents itself.

The next day could have been a full day of fishing, but oddly enough both of us wanted to explore upstream. We had heard of Bone Valley Creek and Sugar Fork Creek, and we wanted to see them and the campsites at their mouths. So we walked, carrying our fishing gear with us.

Most fly fishermen, including us, have a vest or chest pack that holds all our line, clippers, and fly boxes. If there's some sort of large compartment on the back, then the snacks, water bottle, and rain jacket go in there. I prefer the traditional fishing vest because it's so... traditional. However, these vests tend to have lots of small pockets for your stuff, but not much in the way of large storage space for the rain jacket and food. When I stupidly lost my vest (and flies and clippers and...everything except my rod and reel) on the Hiwassee River a few years ago, I bought a combination chest pack and backpack. I don't like the look and feel of it as much as a vest, but it's perfectly suited for Smokies fishing – you do a lot of walking and can end up several miles from where you started. In this kind of fishing you need to have food, water, and a rain jacket with you because you probably won't get back to your base until the end of the fishing day, or in my case, nap time.

We hiked and fished our way up Hazel Creek, and five miles above Proctor we came to Sugar Fork Creek coming in from the west. This campsite fits my style because it has the backcountry feel that Proctor doesn't have, it provides easy access to two fine creeks, and horses are not allowed. I like horses as much as the next guy, and I like the tradition of a pack trip, but they can turn a rock and dirt campsite into a fly-infested mud pit pretty quickly. Although, this isn't as big a problem as you might expect, probably because most horse trips are day trips. I've never actually *seen* a horse at a backcountry site, and I rarely see them on the trail.

There's another, less obvious reason why I like this spot – it has history. This is Horace Kephart country, and if you want to become more familiar with the human side of the Smokies, you have to learn about Horace Kephart.

Here's the short version. Kephart was a bright, educated writer and librarian. He spent his childhood on the Iowa farming frontier during the 1860s and 70s, during which time he developed a great love of the outdoors and outdoor adventures. However, being a bright kid, he pursued an educated, responsible, civilized life in the east, serving as a librarian at Rutgers, Yale, and St. Louis, during which time he wrote articles on outdoor skills for several magazines. About the time he turned 40 he developed what all the books call "health problems," which resulted in separation from his wife and kids. To regain his health, in 1904 he went in search of "a big primitive forest where I could build up strength anew and indulge my lifelong fondness for hunting, fishing, and exploring new ground." What we have here is a classic case of a mid-life crisis, exacerbated by a dependence on alcohol. The health he sought to regain was, I'm guessing, sobriety and the adventure that a settled, urban, family life had squeezed out of him. If he had been born 100 years later, he would have bought a Harley and headed west. Instead, he hopped on a train and headed east, to the heart of the Smoky Mountains.

Having had at least one mid-life crisis myself, I can say with confidence that it's a crisis for the guy going through it, but it can be a catastrophe for all the other people in his life because they are the ones who have to put up with him. So it's possible that Kephart's wife was relieved to see him go, especially since alcohol was involved. I can't accurately judge the situation because I don't know the details, but more importantly, I have learned that none of us are perfect, myself included, and it's not my job to judge others even if I do know the details. Be that as it may, I'd agree with Horace in one respect: spending time in the mountains can help.

So that's what he did. He headed to the last, great, eastern mountain wilderness in 1904. He gained access to a small, abandoned mining cabin about 2½ miles up Sugar Fork's confluence with Hazel Creek, and there he stayed for a little over a year. At that time, the small community of Medlin rested at the confluence, where the Sugar Fork campsite now sits. Medlin consisted of a church/school, a mill, two stores, about half a dozen houses, and a post office, serving about 40 scattered households, including Kephart. It sounds like a Thoreau at Walden Pond kind of thing, but Kephart was more anthropologist than philosopher. He did write a book from this experience, but it was not so much a reflection on life and nature as it was a description of the mountain people, especially the moonshiners and bear hunters. His book, *Our Southern Highlanders*, is still sold in local bookstores.

And this place is still isolated. The quickest route to it is the path Greg and I took: paddle about 3 miles across Fontana, then hike about 5 miles. Or, you can park at the Clingmans Dome parking lot on the main crest, hike about four miles west on the AT, then hike about 12 miles from Silers Bald down Hazel Creek. Oh, and by the way, when you are finished, you'll have to hike back *up* those 16 miles to your car. Or you can start at Fontana Dam and hike about 12 miles across Shuckstack, Eagle Creek, and Jenkins Ridge to Proctor, then hike five miles up Hazel Creek to Sugar Fork. Yep, this place was isolated in 1904, and it still is today. Although, there are a couple of other good, lonely campsites and fishin' holes that I'm not going to mention for fear of alienating my few, remaining fishing partners. I need them, to split the costs on our road trips.

Greg and I fished and hiked our way up to Bone Valley Creek where we found the Bone Valley backcountry campsite and, a bit up Bone Valley Trail, an old cabin with a small cemetery down a trail behind it. My trail guidebook tells me that this was the home of the Hall family, built around 1880, and is the most remote historic building in the park. If it weren't a federal offense (accompanied by a steep fine and possible prison time), sleeping in this old cabin would be high on my To Do list.

Back in the early 1930s, while families were still living in log cabins, growing vegetables, raising livestock and chickens, making moonshine, and getting their mail from post offices in Medlin and Proctor, this Hazel Creek river system became known as a paradise for gentlemen sportsmen. Ritter logging company had finished operations and sold most of their land to several wealthy families in 1929, and several exclusive hunting and fishing clubs were established on Hazel and its tributaries. They stocked these rivers with rainbow trout to replace the devastated populations of native brook trout. As I write this, I don't know how far up Bone Valley Creek you have to go before you get into brookies, but I aim to find out in the next year or two. (In case you are wondering, I *do* know how far up Sugar Fork you have to go to find them. Not far.)

The 1930s and early 40s were probably good years for Hazel Creek and these wealthy families. The logging had stopped, so the valley lost some jobs and some of the poor families probably suffered, but most of those who stayed would have reverted to full-time farming and moonshining. During this time the forests were recovering and the wealthy sportsmen were undoubtedly taking care of the land, to support their hunting and fishing habits. This Hazel Creek valley had a rough two or three decades, starting in the late 1800s, and the residents had seen a flurry of activity and money. The 1930s probably seemed like a return to normalcy, which some would have welcomed and others would not. However, it was during this decade that the state and federal governments began spending several million dollars buying thousands of separate parcels of land to piece together this thing that would come to be known as Great Smoky Mountains National Park.

The original boundary of the park when FDR dedicated it in 1940 was about three or four miles north of Medlin. Bone Valley and Hazel Creek were not part of the park until 1944 when Fontana Lake filled and cut this section off from the rest of the world. According to the TVA, over one thousand families were evicted from the coves of Eagle, Hazel, and Forney Creeks. The only ones who remained were those buried in the small family cemeteries in Proctor, Bone Valley, and dozens of other sites scattered along the north shore of Fontana Lake.

And in case you're wondering, Bone Valley was named for a herd of dead cows. They were being herded up to some open pasture on the ridge tops in the early 1900s (I'd guess Spence Field or Thunderhead) when they were caught by a snowstorm. Probably May, maybe April. Surely not March, because anyone who has spent any time around the Smokies knows that March is one of the worst − no, let's say *unpredictable* − months. Backpackers call it the wild card month because anything can happen in March. You'll have a warm, sunny day followed by a foot of snow the next. By late April you think warm weather is here to stay, and you'd be about 90% right, but that other 10% could kill you if you're a cow on your way to a high mountain pasture.

Hazel is a beautiful place, but honestly, no prettier than a hundred other river valleys in the Smokies. I do have my favorite places in the Smokies, and beauty is part of the equation, but usually the factors that make some places more special than others are things like history and isolation. To me, that's what sets places like Hazel Creek apart from the rest, that's why I keep going back, and that's why I'm telling you about it. You're welcome.

Chapter 5
Long Rod, Short Cast

Keith was in full-blown Chihuahua mode. "Come on, Hoov, get up!" he said, as he scurried around the tent on all fours, trying to find his clothes.

"I told you last night, I'm not getting up at dawn" was my only response.

"You sissy. We came to fish, so let's fish. Get up. It's the least you can do."

"No," I said as I wormed my way deeper into my sleeping bag. "*This* is the least I can do."

I don't know why most of my closest friends are 10 to 15 years younger than I am, but it's times like this – sunrise on a summer morning in the Smokies – that make me wish they were all 10 years older than me. These young whippersnappers are wearing me out.

Chihuahua mode. I've never had a dog like this and never will. When their owner walks into their house, the dog (it's always a small, high-pitched, squeaky dog) gets so excited that he runs around in circles, slipping and sliding and barking. This moment of frenzy is often accompanied by some peeing on the floor – by the dog, I mean. My main fishing partners, Keith Oakes, Tim Landefeld, and Greg Harrell call that "Chihuahua mode," a condition afflicting Keith, the most excitable of the bunch when it comes to fishing. He'll jump out of the truck and into his waders, dash to the river, fish from dawn to dusk without food and water, without a nap, putting all bodily functions on hold. It would be a super-human feat, if it weren't so annoying.

Actually, it doesn't annoy all of us, just the ones who like to sleep late, take naps on the river bank, stop and eat, watch birds, and just generally relax. In other words, it irritates *me*. I'd like to say it's an outlook that comes from wisdom and experience, but there are some who suggest that it's old age. Whatever. Tomayto, Tomahto.

So, Keith was in Chihuahua mode and would not relent until we both were on the river. I consider that to be a sacrifice on my part, an accommodation to the young and restless. Keith sees it as a compromise. It was a cool morning in early summer, and it's my belief that the fish normally won't start biting until mid-morning. That's usually the case, but as Keith is quick to remind me: "Of course you don't catch fish until 10 o'clock, that's when you finally get your lazy butt in the river." Unlike most of our disagreements, in this one instance his logic was irrefutable, so I joined him on the river around 8 am.

Keith and I both started with.... Okay, I don't really remember exactly what we used, but I'm sure we started with dry flies. In warm weather, we always start with dries, either an Elk Hair Caddis, or a Parachute Adams, or a Thunderhead. In the Smokies, it very rarely matters what fly pattern you use because the trout will either cooperate or they won't. It's what the books call "opportunistic." The aquatic insect life is not very abundant in Smokies streams, so the fish will eat pretty much anything that floats by, unless they are not eating at all which happens much more often than I think it should.

The paucity of aquatic insect life is baffling to many because as soon as you set foot in a Smokies visitor center or read the NPS literature, you'll be told about the incredible diversity and abundance of life in the Smokies – wildflowers, trees, insects, amphibians. All that is true as far as it goes, but it doesn't extend to the aquatic insects that trout eat.

By "aquatic insects" we mean those insects that spend a significant portion of their lives in the water, in this case the rivers. I'm not an entomologist, so I don't know all of the insects in the rivers of the Southern Appalachians. However, being one who fishes for trout with a fly rod, I do know a little bit about the main insects that trout eat: mayflies, caddisflies, midges, and stoneflies. These insects have several phases that they pass through, the first being the "nymph" stage. During this stage they look like small roaches or earwigs, living under water, usually under rocks, in gravel, or in sand. After a year or two in this phase, they will one day swim en mass to the surface (or crawl to the shore), their nymphal body will split open and a winged adult will break free. This winged adult will pop through the surface film of the water, float along for several seconds or several minutes as its wings dry out and unfold. This is the point at which they are trout candy.

In many, many rivers around the US it is important that the fly fisherman be well-versed in the subtleties of the life cycle of each of these types of insects, including the various species, such as March Brown, Quill Gordon, Light Cahill, Little Green Caddis, Little Black Caddis, Blue Winged Olives, etc. In the Smokies, there are some occasions when this detailed knowledge is necessary, but those moments are rare. Instead, the fish are hungry, and they are not picky. They'll eat whatever insect floats by. The reasons, ultimately, are the speed and acidity of the water.

The aquatic insects that inhabit trout streams flourish in slightly alkaline water. Unfortunately, the underlying rock and soil composition of southeastern mountain streams creates a somewhat acidic water environment, one that is not conducive to the mayflies, caddis, and stoneflies that trout focus on. Thus, the insect populations in Smokies streams are diverse, but not large. The fish are not well-fed.

Acid rain, which once was a well-publicized threat but is now rarely spoken of, worsens this aquatic situation. The National Parks Conservation Association has reported that rainfall in the Smokies is 5 to 10 times more acidic than clean rain, the highest level of acidity of all our national parks. And it's not just rain. Clouds and fog hanging over Clingmans Dome have occasionally been found to be more acidic than vinegar. Without listing more statistics, let's just say it's not a pretty picture. This isn't good news for humans who visit. It's even worse news for the aquatic insects and fish that need an alkaline environment. The situation isn't drastic because moving water tends to cleanse itself, but movement can't work miracles. Upsetting the ph balance of the water will reduce insect populations and ultimately harm the fish. The result, to be brief, is hungry fish.

The other reason that the fish in the Smokies are opportunistic is much less complicated. It's the rough, fast, bubbly water in the rivers. This kind of water has a lot of dissolved oxygen, which is good for aquatic insects and the fish. However, there are less algae and decomposed leaves in fast moving water; that's less food for the insects which the trout eat. The result is fewer insects and hungry fish. Fortunately, the fish don't usually have the luxury of carefully examining a drifting insect because the insects tend to bounce and swirl and float quickly past. The fish have to make split-second decisions, and that's good news for the fisherman.

The stereotypical view of fly fishing is that one stands in the river, waiting for the expected "hatch" of aquatic insects which will jump-start a feeding frenzy by the fish. These hatches are fairly predictable: Blue Winged Olives in very early spring, Quill Gordons in early spring, Hendricksons in mid spring, Sulphurs in late spring, Light Cahills in summer, and caddises and stoneflies just about any time. Some fly fishers who are particularly clued in to the rhythms of the seasons will use the local plant life as their guide: Blue Winged Olives hatch when the daffodils start blooming, Quill Gordons when the forsythia bushes are blooming, etc. I've never heard of anyone using the astronomical constellations as an indicator of mayfly hatches, but I suspect some have tried: "When you no longer see Orion's belt at midnight, then you'll know the Quill Gordons are taking flight" or something like that. This sounds like advice you'd find in a Farmer's Almanac that predicts the weather a year in advance, which makes me a bit skeptical.

As much as I'd like to believe such home-spun wisdom, I wouldn't bother pursuing the astronomical side of aquatic insect behavior, mainly because it amounts to the same thing as choosing a specific date on the calendar. Orion's belt is going to disappear over the horizon at midnight every year on the same date. On average in the long run, this calendar approach to insect behavior "works," but only in the same way that averages "work." For instance, we can have six inches of rainfall this month by having a consistent drizzle for four weeks, or we can have four weeks of drought interrupted by a few downpours. Both months show up as "six inches" in the record books – just a couple of average months. Likewise, if you head to the Smokies on March 10 hoping the Quill Gordons are hatching, in warm years you'll be late, in cold years you'll be early, and in average years you'll hit it perfectly; assuming, of course, there is such a thing as an average year. It's possible to *never* have an average year.

On the other hand, the flora-based approach does make sense to me. The heavens are not in tune with the local weather variations, but the plants are. If winter lingers, the forsythia and daffodils will hesitate, just as water temperatures in the mountains will be slow to warm and the insects will wait to emerge. An early spring will kick all those inter-related biological processes into gear a bit early. Most of us assume that air and water temperatures are the key factors in this plant/insect/fish awakening, and that's probably true. If length of day is also a factor, then we hope that it affects the plants, insects, and fish in the same fashion. And it probably does. So, yes, go ahead and use the local plants as your guide.

I trust the forsythia bushes around town and the sea gulls on Cherokee Lake. I don't trust the daffodils. These small, yellow flowers are just too, too gullible. Two or three mild days will trick them into blooming, even in the middle of February, when spring is still several weeks away. Forsythia bushes, on the other hand, need a bit more convincing before they burst into bloom. When they begin showing their bright yellow flowers, I know the Hepaticas and Spring Beauties are blooming in the lower elevations of the Smokies and the water temperatures in my favorite Smokies creeks is about 50 degrees, which is when the Quill Gordons begin hatching and the trout start taking notice.

This is also when the Ring-billed Gulls disappear from Cherokee Lake, which is a solid sign of spring, I think. When the plants make a mistake and bloom too early, some of their flowers may get stung by the frigid temperatures, but it's not life threatening. Sea gulls, on the other hand, must be absolutely certain that the time to head north has really come. Theirs is a life-or-death commitment, sort of like the bacon on your breakfast plate. A chicken in a coop made a small sacrifice to provide your eggs. The bacon, on the other hand, took the full commitment of a pig.

Now that I've said all that, I guess I don't have an astronomically or biologically-based system, other than *my* biology maybe. Around the first of March my fishing mojo starts coming out of hibernation, and I head to the Little River near Elkmont campground in the park. I don't watch Orion. I don't watch the calendar. I *notice* the forsythia bushes, but I don't *watch* them. I just go because the weather is becoming enjoyable and my work schedule sometimes permits it. I believe it was Robert Traver who, when asked about the best time to go fishing, responded, "When you can." Yeah, I guess that about sums it up. Most of us go when our schedules allow, and when the weather becomes pleasant. Maybe that's pretty much the system the insects and fish use, too.

There is one other factor in our natural environment that should be considered… livestock. I live in rural east Tennessee, and the local farmers swear (and I believe them) that when the weather man says it's going to snow, ignore him, but when the cows and horses say it's going to snow, "well, by dingy, hit's gonna snow." Animals are in tune with those rhythms of nature that are invisible to us. Cows are predictable. They congregate together in the same places and the same times. They get noisy at the same time in the morning. When they deviate from these patterns, the weather is about to change. Likewise, watch the horses for signs of rain or snow. They get restless, turning around in their stalls or stomping on the ground, as a low-pressure front approaches. I think I've noticed that birds at our bird-feeder do the same thing. And, most importantly, the fish become more active.

I've even heard about research that was done on predicting earthquakes in which they examined newspapers in an area that was hit by an earthquake. The number of "lost dog" reports had increased immediately before the earthquake hit. I don't know if earthquakes make the trout feed, so this might not be useful information for fishing purposes. On the other hand, if a lot of lost dog posters appear on telephone poles in your neighborhood, go buy some bread and milk and head to your panic room. Or, go fishing. In the name of science.

So the stereotypical view of fly fishing involves an insect hatch and fish coming to the surface to eat the insects as they linger at or on the surface. The most unusual aspect of fishing in the Smokies is that you rarely cast to rising fish. The insect hatches are sporadic and light. You spend most of your time casting to likely looking places – behind rocks, along seams, and in the "sweet spots" in the current where the current speed is not too fast and not too slow. I don't know what that speed is in feet-per-second. All I know is that after you've caught some fish in these currents, you'll intuitively know where the right spot is by the speed of your fly's float. You'll cast up in the current, thinking "too fast, too fast…Okay, perfect, now, now…" and you'll either get a strike right then and there, or you'll get nothing because you've floated past the sweet spot in the current.

Another productive spot is the dead water right behind a rock. Fishing these spots with a dry fly is either really easy or really hard, depending on how you look at it. You can't usually cast to these spots because there are currents on both sides of the rock and below the dead spot. Any line on the water will get caught in the current and yank the fly abruptly out of the dead spot. Occasionally, a fish will get excited as he sees the fly jerk across the surface, and he'll strike. He'll usually miss your escaping fly, but every now and then you'll catch him. Nevertheless, don't make this a regular technique. Catching a fish in this manner is the exception, not the rule. Instead, your best bet in these dead water situations is to reach your fly rod out over the dead spot and simply dangle and dance your fly around in the dead spot with little or no line on the water. It's not an aesthetically pleasing style, but it's a method that's worked for many, many years.

As the 19th century drew to a close, Bud had a good life on Sugar Fork, but he hadn't realized it until recently. He was too busy scratching out a living in these mountains to think much about whether he enjoyed his life and whether he would like to live some other way in some other place. Thoughts like that were just idle musings, not good for nothing. The good Lord sets you in a place and that's where you are. So you do what you have to do to feed your family and fulfill your debts to your neighbors. A few years ago, when Bud was a boy, he had almost died of consumption. When his ma and pa got sick too, their neighbors had tended to his family. That's what neighbors do in hard times.

Most years were hard in one way or another. A summer too hot. A winter too cold. A man could handle that. He had to. God sends troubles along the way in every man's life. He has His reasons. It's a man's duty to accept the Lord's blessings and His curses. That's just the way life is.

But now things were different. It wasn't just God's doings, it was man's. Mr. Adams had bought 200 acres on Sugar Fork and was setting up a copper mine. Even worse, Taylor and Crate loggers had built dams on Hazelnut Creek and were cutting down the trees. And wherever they cut, the land and the animals got hurt. Bud's pa had worked for Taylor and Crate for awhile, until he got hurt skidding logs down the mountain. After that he went back to farming and moonshining. That's what he was best at anyways. Now Bud and his pa worked together, on their own schedule, not the lumber company's. They raised corn, beans, and squash, just like the Cherokees had when this was their land. They also raised a few cattle, herding them up Jenkins Ridge every summer to the pastureland high up on Spence Field.

Now most of Hazelnut Creek was ruined for fishing, and there was talk of logging further up all the way to Sugar Fork and beyond. It wouldn't be long before a man couldn't take his son to the creek and show him how to catch a brook trout, because there wouldn't be any left. But today Bud couldn't worry about the future. He would spend a few hours on Sugar Fork, catching some fish for supper. And so Bud took his cane pole and went to the river.

Bud decided to go downstream. He didn't feel like having to be social if any of the neighbor kids saw him. But downstream, the first half mile of the stream, was the best water. So, Bud headed east, down the valley of the Sugar Fork on the eastern slope of Jenkins Ridge.

It was late spring and the creek was still full from the spring rains. That would make the fishing a little easier. The fishing was hardest in late summer and early fall, when the water was low and slow and clear, and the fish would shy away from any little movement above them. Last night's light rain had discolored the water just a tad, making Bud's prospects even better still. The fish would be able to see his lure make a dent on the water's surface, but would not be able to see all the details clearly. It was last night's rain – not too heavy – that had convinced Bud that today would be a good day to fish. A man couldn't do that working for the lumber company.

Bud's cane pole was twice as long as he was tall. He loved the feel of it in his hands. It was a tool, like an ax or a hoe, but in the hands of an experienced mountain man, it was more than a tool. It was a magical wand that could conjure up a tasty trout from the river bed. Some people could see the fish in the clear-as-moonshine waters of Sugar Fork. Bud had never developed that skill, but he still caught plenty of fish. A man didn't have to see the fish to catch them, just as long as the fish didn't see him. It didn't take long for a fella to learn where the fish would lie – behind the rocks, at the tail ends of the sluices between the rocks, or at the swirling bottom of a deep pool.

Bud arrived at a small plunge pool that should have some fish. He'd fished here often. Last fall he caught a mess of trout using live grasshoppers as bait. The fishing that day had been easy. The hardest part had been catching the grasshoppers.

He hid behind a tree, surveying the water. He sometimes worked his way downstream, hiding behind the rocks above deep pools, stretching his pole over the white water below. On those days he could catch fish by tying a yaller hammer or cardinal feather to his hook and letting the current pull the lure downstream beneath the surface. He'd sometimes see the underwater flash of white and orange as a speckled trout attacked the lure, but most of the time he'd simply wait for the tug on his tight line.

Today he would work upstream so that he would come up behind the fish, since they would be facing upstream looking for bugs to come floating down to them. He often fished this way during the "bug season" of April and May. His pole was long enough that Bud often didn't even get his feet wet, but on a hot day he would gladly wade waist deep in the cold water. It was those moments that made Bud feel truly alive.

Bud bent down low and approached the river. He had about 10 feet of string on the end of his pole, and at the end of his string he had a hook with a bit of rabbit fur tied on and a tiny feather wrapped around it. It didn't look to Bud like the bugs that sometimes floated in the surface of the water, but the fish seemed to be attracted to the shape and movement rather than the details. Sometimes he'd fish like this because he didn't feel like digging for grubs or catching grasshoppers. Sometimes, especially in the spring, catching fish with a fur-and-feather lure was almost easy. Truth be told, Bud somewhat enjoyed catching fish this way. It was a nice change of pace, but most important, it worked. Sometimes.

He pointed his pole downstream and slowly swung it around so that it pointed across the creek and a few feet behind the spot in the current where the fish would be. He held it still for a moment. It looked like a tree branch hanging over the river. The string and feather-and-fur lure at the end was almost invisible, dangling downstream, bouncing on the surface. Sometimes his lure's dance on the surface would look like a bug skittering on the surface and a fish would strike.

With a slight twitch of his wrists, Bud flicked his light-as-air lure upstream into the current. As the lure floated downstream Bud raised his pole to keep his line off the water. Once the lure had passed under the tip of his pole, Bud's expectations for a fish were almost gone. Any fish downstream from him would probably have seen the movement of his pole. Nevertheless, Bud lowered his pole to give more line to allow his lure to float a little farther. Sometimes a desperate fish would take his lure during this downstream drift. At the end of the drift, when the line was tight, Bud would let his lure dance on the surface far downstream, just in case a fish wanted a dancing fly instead of a floating fly.

But nothing happened, so Bud tried it again. He'd usually give each sluice two or three chances before moving on. So he again flipped his lure upstream and watched as it bounced along on the surface like a helpless insect. It took only one second for the lure to move several feet downstream. "The trout would not be there," thought Bud, "the water is too fast." As the lure continued its brief journey, the flow became slower and flatter, becoming more of a long, moving swirl than a series of bumps. "That's the spot. That's where he'll...." Before Bud had finished his thought, the trout struck at the lure. "This is a good sign. The fish will work with me today." Bud always knew within the first 5 or 10 minutes whether the fish could be caught that day, or not. Today they could.

The fight was brief and uneventful because the fish was small, as they usually were in these high elevations. Bud had never had the chance to fish in a larger river, down in the valleys. The lumber companies had either dammed them up or dirtied them up. The brook trout just couldn't live like that, and Bud understood. He couldn't live like that either. His pa had told him of the old days on lower Hazelnut Creek and the Little Tennessee River. The fishin' in the old days was better than now. Bud sometime wondered if that was really true. It seemed like the old folks always remembered big about the past. But, as Bud thought about the copper mines and the lumber companies, and their move up the rivers and creeks, he feared that someday he would tell his children how there used to be fish in Sugar Fork, and a man with a bamboo pole could catch fish all day when the creek was full and water was a bit colored from a sparse rain.

Bud put the fish in his flour sack. It wasn't big – about as long as a man's hand – but it was big enough to keep.

Bud could float his fly again in the same run to see if there were more fish, but because he was confident today, he simply moved on to another spot. Only when he was desperate would he try a good spot over and over. Bud had thought about this and wondered if, in desperate moments when the fish weren't biting, he should give up on a barren spot quickly or whether he should stay in that one spot longer. The old timers had different opinions on that question. Bud usually would stay in one spot, not because he was convinced by the old timers who said he should, but because it's just hard to walk away from a good-looking fishing hole, even if there's one just as good just a stone's throw up the river.

Bud's next target was a small piece of dead water behind a rock about the size of a frying pan. It was a bit upstream and off toward the near bank. Bud took only a few steps upstream and raised his rod tip high above the frying pan rock. He let it down slowly until his feather and fur deception barely touched the dead water. Then he began the dance of the lure. He swirled the lure around the surface in a circle and then a figure 8. Some men swore by the figure 8 pattern; others said it didn't matter. Bud sided with the "doesn't matter" men, and so he was free to use whatever pattern struck his fancy. On some days, he would spell out his real name, Isaac, which worked well, perhaps because it had so many round shapes, like a figure 8. On other days, he would just bounce and dance the lure in circles and jerks like a Saturday night dance. Today he was confident, so he knew it wouldn't matter.

And it didn't matter, because there was no fish there. Or else the fish that was there wasn't interested. Bud danced his lure until his outstretched arms got tired of holding the pole over the water. And Bud began to doubt. He knew that it was unusual to catch a fish on every try, but the first one had been so easy, and the creek was full, and it had rained last night. But he began to lose confidence. Maybe his first fish would be his only fish. Maybe there was only one easy fish in the river, and he had stumbled upon him early. Maybe...

"All right. Let's try 'er again," thought Bud. He stepped knee-deep into the water and reached farther across to another rock on the other side of the main channel. "This time, it's the figure 8. It might not matter, but if it does, it's the figure 8 that'll work." And so, Bud's lure danced its little dance, Bud's pole tip held high, the magic wand creating a fish out of water, rock, and gravel. And it worked. The fish struck and was hooked. It was a bigger fish than the first. Bud's string was not new, so he'd be gentle. "No need to hurry; but not too long and slow. Just tire him out a little. Let him jump." Which he did. Three quick jumps in rapid succession, like a panicked deer leaping through thick grass. A blur of brown-orange, with a hint of white. A fish out of water, in the air. He was more than food for Bud. At that moment he was a challenge. A part of God's creation attached by a string and a piece of bamboo to another, larger part of God's creation. Connected, for just a few moments. One's life dependent on the other's death. It was a drama played out hundreds of times every day in the mountains. Trout and mayflies. Foxes and mice. Hawks and snakes. Bud and trout.

The trout swam to the bottom and shook. Bud enjoyed this part as much as he enjoyed the jumps and cartwheels. There is an indescribable sense of mystery in feeling, in knowing, that something alive is at the end of the line, fighting for its life... and then the fight was over. After a moment of admiring the cold, glowing beauty of the fish in the gravel, the fish became merely food, tonight's meal. Into the flour sack.

A fish might spend his whole life in a small area no bigger than a man's bed. Bud sometimes felt like a trout. He had spent his whole life on Sugar Fork and Hazelnut Creek. God had put Bud on Sugar Fork, and that's where he'd live his life. God had put a trout behind that rock, and that's where that trout would live his life – until a man came along to take him away from his home.

Sixty years later, when Bud was an old man living near Bryson City, his home on Sugar Fork having been used by Ritter logging company and later bought by the government, he would think about this day, and he would remember that trout, and he would remember the men in dark suits with official papers who had taken Bud from his home, forever.

The old-timers used a cane pole – maybe 8 or 10 or even 12 feet – with about that many feet of line on the end. They would "fly fish" by dragging one or two flies or three flies downstream, underwater or by reaching their pole out over the water and dancing their fly in these dead spots. Some preferred to jump the fly up and down, some just let it sit with an occasional twitch, others preferred a figure eight pattern. This is one of those debates that probably never made it onto the printed page.

I've never fished for Smokies' trout with a 12 foot cane pole. I've thought about it, but then I decided I've come pretty close to doing it already. Here comes one of those Smoky Mountain fly fishing debates that *has* made it onto the printed page: long rod vs. short rod. Some fly fishers prefer the short rod because you'll have less chance of snagging your fly on your backcast, because your line will be a foot or two closer to you. Therefore, use a rod that's 6 or 7 feet long. The other side, the long rodders, says you should use a rod that's about 9 feet long because it enables you to lift the tip higher to keep more line off the water – an important detail when fishing a stream full of broken, conflicting currents. You can even use your long rod like the old-timer's cane pole, just reaching out and dangling your fly behind the rocks. I'm on the long rodders side of the debate, possibly for some subconscious Freudian reasons, but mainly because of the cane pole technique, and the fact that I mostly fish on the lower, larger rivers where there's more room for a backcast. You just can't reach out and dangle your fly behind rocks with a short rod, thus missing about half of the holding spots on many of these mountain rivers. Although, in typical fly fisherman fashion, I've managed to negotiate a perfectly obvious solution... buy a 7 foot *and* a 9 foot rod. I use the long rod on larger streams where I do a lot of reaching and dangling. I use the shorter rod when I'm several miles up the river valley, fishing the smaller headwaters that are crowded – sometimes completely enclosed like a tunnel – with rhododendron bushes.

In addition to rod length, there's also the issue of rod *action*. In this, there's no real debate. You definitely must use a limber, slow action rod. Not many rod makers use the word "slow" anymore. I guess it sounds in some way inferior. This is, after all, 21st century America where bigger is better than smaller, and faster is better than slower. But not when fly fishing in small streams where you rarely have to make a cast longer than 25 feet, and 90% of your casts are in the 10 to 15 foot range. As an acquaintance of mine once said, when asked about the right rod for these streams, "It's not how far you can cast. It's how *short*." You want a rod that casts well at 5 to 15 feet. That means you don't want a stiff, fast action rod made for 80 foot casts. Use what manufacturers call a "moderate" or "traditional" action rod, both of which are marketing euphemisms for "slow."

In fact, if you really want to be classy, this is the perfect excuse to buy a bamboo rod. If you are unfamiliar with fly rods, then this might sound like the old timers' cane pole. Nope. The bamboo is specially imported from Asia. It's carefully measured, split, planed, and varnished. It takes a lot of highly skilled labor, and is therefore very expensive. But it's also slow action, full flex, perfect for short, delicate casting in mountain rivers.

There are some fly fishermen who use *only* bamboo fly rods. These folks, through their use of a fly rod made of an organic material, sense a mystical connection to the golden age of fly fishing. They yearn for the days before graphite and fiberglass, to a simpler, gentler time; a time when bamboo was king, and men's hearts were pure. They are making a statement about values, about conservation and consumption, about truth, goodness, and beauty. Or, perhaps the connection is with the earth itself, or the fish, or history, or poetry, or the spirit of the sport. Or maybe not. I don't know, and maybe they don't know either because that's the way mystical connections are. The mystic probably can't explain it, but even if he could, he doesn't owe anyone an explanation. The best explanation I've heard was short and appropriately vague: "A graphite rod has no soul." As a quasi-mystic, that makes sense to me, even though I have no idea what it means.

I'm sorry to say that I don't own a bamboo rod. My view is that if I bought a cheap one, it wouldn't be worth using, and if I bought an expensive one, it would be worth too much to use. You fall down a lot in Smokies rivers, sometimes without enough warning to hold your rod up above your head. I've heard of concussions and broken bones resulting from guys trying to protect their expensive fly rods as they were slipping and sliding on slick river rocks. Such stories sound like accidents, but these guys probably had figured this out ahead of time: medical insurance will pay about 80% of your medical bills but 0% to repair an expensive bamboo rod, so breaking bone instead of bamboo becomes a sensible, financial decision.

All wild trout are beautiful, with their deep, cold colors, but I think the prettiest is the brook trout. Maybe it's the combination of orange, brown, green, and a hint of blue and white. Maybe it's the white edges on their fins. Maybe it's just that I haven't caught enough of them to take them for granted. (Blue jays are outrageously beautiful birds, but I don't stop and stare whenever I see one because they are so common. It's almost a sin to allow yourself to become so jaded.) Whatever the reason, you can still catch these beautiful fish in the higher elevations in the Smokies. In lower elevations, you will catch rainbows and browns. In some streams, you can find a small waterfall that is the dividing line between these populations. Brookies above, rainbows and browns below.

Many years ago, brook trout were the only trout in high elevation Smokies rivers. (Brook trout are scientifically classified as char, not trout, but that doesn't matter to 99.9% of trout fisherman. If something looks like a duck, walks like a duck, and quacks like a duck, it's probably a duck. But even if it's not, you might as well call it one. Brookies look and act like trout. So, I'm callin' them trout, in spite of what the taxonomists say.) Before the park was established in the 1930s, rainbow and brown trout were brought in and stocked in these rivers to replace the decimated brook trout populations, and these newcomers out-competed the few brookies that had survived the trauma of the logging years. The stocking stopped in the 1970s, so all the trout that you catch today in the Smokies are wild, born and raised in the river, but only the brook trout are true natives. They are the trout the pioneers would have caught 150 years ago. The Cherokee Indians would have caught and eaten them 300 years ago. Or the Mississippian Indians 1,000 years ago. Or the Woodland Indians 2,000 years ago. Brookies are "native" in the best and oldest sense of the word.

Another fact of life that disappoints many people: the fish are small. Perhaps we should wait a moment for that reality to settle in.

Ready to continue? Okay, keep this in mind: context matters. After you've caught several 6 to 8 inch rainbows, that 10 inch fish that you catch will look stout. Twelve inches is a monster. Sixteen or larger (and there are a few of these larger ones in the deep pools, caught almost exclusively by deep-water nymph fishermen) is the fish of a lifetime. I'm not saying you'll catch a 12 or 16 inch fish. I'm just saying that context matters. These are small, beautiful mountain streams. The fish are, in the words of John Gierach, "exactly the size that they're supposed to be, no more and no less." Some people would say this is merely lowering your expectations, and I guess I would agree because lowering one's expectations may be the secret to a happy life. Think about your job and finances, or your weight, or your teenagers, or the sports that you used to enjoy playing. Exactly... lowering your expectations. Or, if you prefer euphemisms: adjusting one's expectations to an appropriate level. So why should fishing be any different?

It's been said that one of the charms of trout fishing is that the trout live in such beautiful places: the Yellowstone River, the Snake River, the Hiwassee River, and, of course, over a hundred miles of streams in the Great Smoky Mountains. That's context, too. And it's a big part of fishing for trout, of *why* we fish for trout. Beautiful surroundings can make ordinary fishing seem extraordinary, because it's about more than just catching big fish.

There will be some days that you'll fish in the Smokies and get skunked. Not even a strike. You'd swear there's not a fish in the river. It's on days like this that Keith and I will look at each other and say, sarcastically, "Well, it's just good to be out" or "It's better than being at work." Both those clichés are, of course, true, but the reality is that we've just gotten a good ol' Smoky Mountain butt-kicking. All the platitude-laden conversation about it just being "good to be out" can't erase the fact that we've been outsmarted by a bunch of 7 inch creatures with brains the size of a pea. We couldn't find a single fish in the whole river that was stupider than we are. That happens more often than I'd like to admit.

Over the years I've learned that there are only a few ways to catch trout with a fly rod and dozens of ways that *don't* work. So I habitually try those dozens of ineffective methods to see if they still don't work, and based on my experience, they still don't. But – and I'll say this with a straight face because I really do believe it – it really was just good to be out, waist-deep in a beautiful river. And that really is why I fish for trout in the Smokies, because it's a way of not just watching nature but of participating in it; to not simply observe but to immerse yourself in the natural world. You become for a few hours a predator, like a heron or an otter or a bear. For a few hours, this is your home. It is where you belong. And if you catch a few fish, so much the better.

Chapter 6
Sunrise, Sunset, And Then Some

"Hey, Hoov. I want to hike the eastern half of the Smokies. Are you free two weeks from Friday?"

I had some commitments on that Saturday and Sunday, so I simply responded, "Naw. I can't." And that was the end of the conversation.

A couple of days later Keith asked again, "Are sure you can't get free the day after Thanksgiving?"

"Friday, maybe, but Saturday and Sunday, I can't."

Keith's quick comeback caught me off guard. "Great, then let's do it!"

I paused for a moment, confused. "I can't, man. I'm tied up on the weekend."

Keith persisted, "That's not a problem."

At this point I was beginning to feel like I was trapped in an Abbot and Costello *Who's on First* routine. Neither one of us seemed to know what the other was talking about.

Keith continued, "You'll only be gone for a day."

"A day?" A pause as I let the meaning of his last statement sink in. "Are you talking about hiking 30 miles of the AT in one day?"

Keith corrected me. "Thirty-one miles, actually. Plus the trail to Cammerer."

We had now stepped out of the Abbot and Costello routine and into the *Twilight Zone*. Rod Serling suddenly appeared, stood in the corner of the room, cigarette in hand, and said: "Two men – one young and eager, the other not. Their lives, stable and routine, will soon be tested by circumstances over which they have no control. For you see, they are about to enter an outdoor world not of their own making. Another world, a different place and a different time. Some know it as the Smoky Mountains, but *we* know it by a different name. We know it as a place where night is day and day is night. Where reason gives way to enthusiasm. A place known simply as... the twilight zone." Puff on cigarette. Cue the music.

I had once read of a guy who did the entire eastern half of the Smokies back in the 1930s. It took him close to 18 hours. The thought of hiking from Newfound Gap along the main ridge crest to Davenport Gap on the northeastern end of the park was intriguing, if not a bit misguided and unrealistic. So, of course, I agreed immediately. It sounded like a trip perfectly suited for a guy who occasionally feels the need to prove his manhood; although, there was a certain element of risk involved – the risk of failure and, therefore, *dis*proving one's manhood. That seems to happen more often than it used to. I can't imagine why.

The most significant risk in this trip would be the length – 31.4 miles. None of us had ever walked that far in a single day, and we didn't really know how long it would take. Our best guess was about 14 or 15 hours on the assumption that we could average about 2 mph, maybe even 2.5. That would be about typical for a day hike, including rest and scenery stops. Of course, there was also the possibility that we would maintain at least a 2 mph speed for the first half, but we might slow significantly in the last half. We simply didn't know because this was all uncharted territory for us. Not the trail itself, but the sheer distance.

Of course, the fact that I used "we" several times in that previous paragraph implies that "we" could hike at the same pace. A dubious assumption, given that one of us was 15 years older than the other, and the other has Chihuahua-like tendencies.

The other problem was daylight. It was late November, and we were a month away from the shortest day of the year, so there seemed to be no way that we could complete the hike in the 11 hours between dawn and dark. Even the most optimistic scenario had us walking several hours in the dark. The only question was how many hours. Of course, waiting until the long days of summer wasn't an option because...well, I suppose it was an option, and a pretty good one, too. However, once we got it into our heads that we were going to do this, we became like kids at Christmas. We got all wiggly and giggly and excited about it and couldn't wait. So – bad idea or not – we'd do it in late November.

So very early on a late November morning, four of us – Keith Oakes, Greg Harrell, Mark Harrell, and I – drove a few miles to the #407 exit off I-40 and continued through Sevierville and Pigeon Forge with impunity. A drive like this – 4 am on a weekday in the off season – can make you feel rather smug at being able to drive quickly down this road which is normally the travelling equivalent of quicksand. You just can't move quickly though Sevierville and Pigeon Forge unless it's a time like this. I imagine it's the same feeling you would get by tiptoeing past a couple of guard dogs who were asleep at their post. You feel like you've pulled something over on someone.

During the drive we traded manly stories, mostly about old hiking injuries and camping blunders, including a number of vomiting and diarrhea incidents. As I recall, it was Mark's fast driving on some winding roads combined with our sausage biscuit breakfast that raised the subject of nausea. I told of my tendency toward car sickness whenever I combined lack of sleep, greasy food, and winding roads. Over the past 30 years I've puked in the early morning hours on all the major roads in the Smokies, a record that will probably never be broken. Mark didn't get the hint and continued to drive under the influence (of caffeine and adrenaline).

The night was cold, clear, and silver-bright as the moon above us lit up the sky, the mountains, and the patches of ice along the sides of the road. We drove up the steep, winding road past familiar landmarks—Sugarlands, the Chimneys, and Alum Cave Trail. This road – US 441 – is known as Newfound Gap Road within the park. At its highest point it crosses the main, state line ridge of the Smokies at Newfound Gap and then continues another 15 miles into the Cherokee Indian Reservation. The Appalachian Trail follows the main ridge crest very closely for almost 72 miles within the park. The eastern half is 31.4 miles and the western half is 40.3.

Not long ago, I was asking an elderly lady for directions to a road in my county. She told me to turn at "the new high school." The only high school I knew of was built in 1976. After a few moments of befuddlement, I realized that's the high school she was talking about. To life-long residents, that high school will always be "the *new* high school." The name Newfound Gap is sort of like that.

An old wagon path across the Smokies used to run pretty much where US 441 runs today, except that it crossed the main ridge crest a couple of miles west at Indian Gap. In the 1850s Arnold Guyot *found a new gap* that was lower than Indian Gap and called it, uncreatively but accurately, Newfound Gap. When the road was being widened and improved in the 1920s, the road was re-routed through Newfound Gap. A thousand years from now, it will probably still be Newfound.

After arriving at Newfound Gap parking lot about 4:45 am, we spent a few minutes pulling our gear and day packs together, taking various items of clothing off and putting others on, then we headed into the woods at 5 am, just to the right of the stone platform where FDR had dedicated the park in 1940, six years after it was actually established. The night gave us perfect conditions for a night hike, something none of us had done before, so we were looking forward to the experience.

A quick look at a calendar showed that the moon would be about ¾ full, which meant that it would shine for about ¾ of the night. Because it was *late* in its cycle, it would shine for the *last* ¾ of the night. In other words, this waning moon would rise about 10 pm and would still be high in the sky when the sun rose and overpowered it. Perfect conditions for a pre-dawn hike. So, we decided to hike a couple of hours before sunrise, under the light of a bright moon.

Relying on the light of a bright moon assumed that we'd have a cloudless night – a fairly safe bet for this season of year, not to mention the fact that we were at the end of one of the driest summers in Tennessee history. And that's exactly what happened – a clear, bright night. All the pieces were falling into place for a great day. The clear sky would give us bright moonlight by night and crisp, panoramic views during the day. Mother Nature was cooperating beyond anything that we deserved. So, of course, we were worried.

We'd all been on enough fishing and hiking trips to have grasped the concept of "paying your dues." You know the idea. If things are going well, just wait, they'll get worse. Or, if things are going badly, they are just balancing out some brief, good fortune you had in the past. And, of course, the good is always in the past, not the future, so that good fortune guarantees something bad will happen, but bad fortune is no guarantee of impending good. So whenever we experience a stroke of good fortune, we go outdoors and engage in some form of self-imposed abuse, hoping for some small degree of control over the hardship that inevitably happens. Yes, it's a sadly pessimistic view of life, but there's substantial evidence to support it.

Sometimes in the cold of January, Keith will get antsy and need to go fishing in one of the nearby rivers. We both know the chances of catching some trout on a fly are pretty slim, and the chances of being warm and dry are even slimmer. On a typical January day, you'll be frozen to the core if the day is clear, or you'll be wet if the temperature is mild. The fish prefer mild and rainy, so that is our preference, too. However, like most folks, it's hard to get away from work, so we fish when we can, not when we'd prefer. So, cold or mild, dry or wet, Keith will call me the night before and say, "Let's go out and pay some dues now so we'll be all paid up when spring gets here." As any fisherman knows, that logic is airtight, so we go to the river to balance our accounts.

Only people with that kind of world view can step onto the trail on a beautiful, crisp, clear morning in the Smoky Mountains and wonder when "it" is going to happen. You know, IT – the sprained ankle or broken leg, the forgotten jacket or lost water bottle, the 33° rain or the iced-over trail. The closest we can get to being optimistic in such circumstances is hoping that whatever "it" is, it will happen on the way home at the *end* of the trip. So we walked into the forest, thrilled but uneasy at such perfect conditions. And, being the oldest one in the group, I probably had the most to be worried about because it's usually the *old* deer in the herd that dies when conditions become harsh.

The AT began an almost immediate ascent. We were, after all, starting in Newfound *Gap*, a gap being a low spot in a ridge. This uphill stretch would take us from 5,000' to about 6,000' at a rate of about 500 feet per mile, typical for a Smokies trail. The trees were mostly spruce and firs. Normally, this would create heavy shade even in the daylight. However, over the last couple of decades, most of the mature fir trees have been killed by the balsam wooly adelgid, a tiny insect imported from Europe that gradually poisons these trees. This has been a terribly sad event in the life of the Smokies, losing some of their most beautiful, distinctive trees. However, if there's an upside to this tragedy, it's that it has opened up the leafy canopy along the AT. The spruce will continue to grow and fill in the canopy while the firs will grow a few years then die, only to be replaced by a new cohort of young firs. The spruce and small firs create that dark, green forest with a Christmas tree smell that we all associate with a northern, balsam forest. In the meantime, walking through a balsam forest under a bright moon is a magical, other-worldly experience consisting of moonshadows interspersed with stretches of silvery moonlight. I think I caught a glimpse of several fauns and hobbits lurking among the trees.

Because the temperature was hovering right around freezing, we started out with jackets, but within 10 minutes we were beginning to shed clothing. The secret to cold weather hiking is to stay one step ahead of the sweat. Wear layers of clothing and begin taking them off as soon as you sense that warm, fuzzy feeling that precedes sweat. I actually spent most of the hike in light nylon pants and a T shirt. It was a bit nippy, but it was the good, invigorating kind of cold that wakes you up and keeps you attentive. It may seem like a cliché to say that it "makes you feel alive," but that really is the best way to say it because that's exactly what it does.

In my opinion, it's not a good idea to wear an insulated vest on cold weather day hikes. I prefer to have sleeves on my jacket because the hiking does exactly what a vest is designed to do – it keeps your core temperature elevated to a safe level, as long as you keep a steady flow of carbohydrates coming in. However, your hands, arms, and ears can get very cold. I often would find myself hiking in light pants, a hat (that I would constantly be taking on and off as the best means of temperature control), a polyester T shirt, and gloves because I'd be completely warm and comfortable, except for my hands and ears.

One thing that had concerned me was the potential for ice on the trail. We all knew from past experience that these first 3 or 4 miles of the AT east of Newfound Gap were a very wet part of the trail. There are numerous springs that seep along the edge of the trail and trickle down the rut of the trail. After an extended cold spell, the trail in several spots becomes a 5 foot wide and 50 foot long patch of ice. With a steep slope to your right and to your left, there's just no way to avoid these slippery spots. So crampons – small spikes strapped to the bottom of your boots – become necessary. For fast easy hiking, the best scenario is no ice – so you don't have to bother with crampons. The second best scenario is lots of ice – so you can put your crampons on and keep them on. The worst scenario is occasional patches of ice – so you have to keep putting the crampons on and taking them off. Generally, in these patchy situations, if you keep your crampons on you'll break or dent them in the ice-free, rocky sections. Luckily for us, the weather had been cold but not yet deeply frigid and wet. There were only a few, small, scattered patches of ice, and we were able to side step most of them. I never took my crampons out of my pack.

There was actually as much ice on the trees as on the trail. On some of the higher spots along the ridge, the remnants of hoarfrost (fog that has frozen in small columns and patterns on objects that are exposed to the open air) from last week's hard freeze clung tenuously to the trees above us. Wind and warmer temperatures sent small chunks of ice clattering through the branches, pelting us as we walked, but not quite melting after they hit the ground.

The hiking order for the day quickly established itself. Greg Harrell in the front with Keith right behind him. I fell in behind them, sometimes just a few yards behind, sometimes a hundred yards or more. Mark Harrell followed me.

Mark was taking his time because he knew from the beginning that he wasn't really ready for this trip. He hadn't exercised in a while, so his legs and lungs probably weren't going to be up to the task. He developed a slow, steady pace as sort of a test to see how he'd hold up. He was the tortoise. Greg and Keith were the hare. I don't know what I was, some sort of old, slow, plodding mammal, I guess. Actually, that's a perfect description of a middle aged man, which is what I am, and I proved it all day long. In fact, by noon Greg and Keith were calling me "the old mule," and I suppose that's a fair appraisal. However, in my defense, I'm also the one most likely to stop and look at scenic panoramas, trees, birds, and other small details along the trail. So, I prefer to describe myself not as slow, just easily distracted.

At first most of our night views were to the south into North Carolina, so we could occasionally see the subtle glow of Bryson City and Cherokee a few miles in the distance. That view to the south is wild and uncivilized because beyond the border of the Smokies lies the rugged, sparsely-populated Nantahala National Forest. (It's the area where Eric Rudolph successfully evaded the FBI for five years.) As the day progressed, we would have many great views of purple ridge after purple ridge stretching to the southern horizon, with no civilization in sight.

Our views to the north into Tennessee were quite different, and that difference became immediately apparent as the AT crossed over to the Tennessee side of the ridge crest. Being night, the gaudy radiance of Pigeon Forge and Sevierville dominated the northern horizon. I suppose it's in some way impressive, but we were in the mountains for a wilderness adventure, and those city lights don't fit in with a wilderness motif. Later in the day, after the sun had risen, the view would improve because during the daylight hours, the tourist havens of Pigeon Forge and Sevierville don't stick out like sore thumbs. In fact, they mostly blend in to the green, hilly landscape. But during our night hike, they made their presence known with a vengeance. As one writer put it, Pigeon Forge is the epitome of "the consumption of fun and the fun of consumption," go-kart tracks and outlet malls, all under a blinding, halogen glow. I tried not to look, fearing I might turn into a pillar of salt.

About 6:15 am we passed the Boulevard, a trail leading north to the top of Mt. Le Conte, and then we passed the Icewater Spring shelter, one of the most heavily-used backcountry campsites in the park. Normally, we would have stopped to rest and snack, but it was dark and there might be some backpackers asleep in it. (There had been one car in the parking lot when we arrived.) We continued on another mile to Charlies Bunion, one of the most dramatic, unique spots in the Smokies. This barren, rocky outcrop was created by a fire in 1925 followed by a heavy rain in 1929 that completely denuded this spot. The result was a rugged, steep, rocky promontory with 360° views. Dawn was breaking as we arrived so we scrambled to the top and witnessed a dramatic sunrise. Schedule-wise we had hoped to be past the Bunion by sunrise, but scenery-wise it was perfect timing. There are numerous places in the park to watch the sun rise or set. None are better than Charlies Bunion. As a bonus, it will usually be an uncrowded event because very few people will hike in the dark. We had Charlies Bunion all to ourselves for those 15 minutes.

This was the point at which Mark decided to go back to the car at Newfound Gap. We had known from the beginning that this might be the best option, but there was no shame and only a little disappointment. He had hiked 4 miles under a clear, moonlit sky in a beautiful place and had witnessed a dramatic sunrise with a few good friends. We should have had cheese and a bottle of champagne. In fact, if we all had gone back to the car, we still could have called the trip a success. I suppose that is the danger in having a great start to such a trip. It would be easy to be satisfied with those first 2 hours. However, a volatile mix of testosterone and peer pressure kept us going. So Mark went west while Keith, Greg, and I went east.

Soon after we parted company it occurred to us that the point of no return had just shifted from the 16 mile point to wherever we happened to be standing at the moment. Mark's return to the car would save us the trouble of having to drive back to Newfound Gap to retrieve the car at the end of the day, but we also realized that the three of us were now fully committed to finishing all 31.4 miles. When he drove his car away, we had at that moment burned our bridges behind us. We couldn't go back now, even if we wanted to – which we didn't.

We now knew that we were averaging about 2 miles per hour. Thus began our debate: how fast should we try to go? Greg lobbied for 3 mph, which is a pace that I could manage on level, paved ground but not in the mountains, and not all day. Keith said we needed to travel *at least* 2.5 mph. I, being the old mule, suggested 2.5 mph at *most*. What we soon discovered was that the debate didn't matter. We'd make the best time we could. Calculating our speed wouldn't help us to get done any faster, but it would give us an idea of when we would get to the end. We didn't know it yet, but our overall speed for the entire day, including rest and scenery stops, would be a little better than 2 mph. Although, I have to admit that Greg and Keith had to wait several times for me to catch up. And, being good friends whose bark is bigger than their bite, they did *have to* wait, because Greg had the only water filter. (If I had been hiking with lesser friends, *I* would have carried the filter to keep them honest.) They would wait patiently for me so that we could all fill our water bottles together. Otherwise, I would have spent the entire day waterless and several miles behind them. This was definitely the "weakest link" principle in action. How long would it take us to finish this 31.4 mile hike? The answer: As long as it takes the slowest member of the group. That would be me.

If you want a nice, solitary hiking experience, hike with someone who walks at a different pace than you, either faster or slower. Not only did we not see a single other person for the entire trip, but we didn't see each other much either. I tried for a while – out of pure peer pressure and male ego – to keep up with Greg and Keith, but I just couldn't do it. Peer pressure can be a powerful motivator, but it can't work miracles. I spent the vast majority of the day walking by myself, which was fine. It added to the wilderness feel of the trip. When we got home and a woman asked me what we talked about all day (a typical female misunderstanding about men), I could not only say that we didn't talk much, I could also say that we hardly even saw each other. Her response was, "Oh, that's too bad." Rather than break into my lecture on gender roles as they relate to male-female differences in conversational styles, I opted for the path of least resistance: I just said, "Yeah" and changed the subject.

It was now daylight as we made our way along the rocky ledges of the Sawteeth, crossing back and forth from the North Carolina to the Tennessee sides of the ridge crest. On the topo map, the Tennessee side of the ridge consists of crowded contour lines, indicating a steep drop into the watershed of the

Middle Prong of the Little Pigeon River. There is a 20 mile portion of ridge stretching from Mt. Le Conte to Mt. Guyot which has no side trails connecting the ridge crest with the area below. The terrain is too rough to build and maintain trails here. Looking down into it from above is a beautiful, raw scene. It's ironic that this rugged, mostly-untouched part of the park has farms, fields, roads, condos, and Pigeon Forge as a backdrop. In retrospect, that semi-civilized background of towns and farms actually accentuates its wildness.

I am happy to report that in spite of the attack of the balsam adelgids, the forest along the ridge crest is still mostly spruce and fir. The firs are all young because they are killed by the balsam adelgid after just a few years. The largest firs I saw were about 20' tall and about 10" in diameter. The spruce, being immune to the adelgids' attack, get much larger. At several spots they were 70' or 80' tall with bare trunk for the lower half and green branches covering the top half, giving a majestic, Western look. Most of the balsam forest, however, has a young, fresh look, but it still has a Canadian look and smell to it. And there are a few places that look old – deep shade, large spruce trees, and thick, green moss on fallen logs. It's not a climax forest yet, but it's moving in that direction.

There are also occasional beech gaps – low spots in the ridge that are small, flat, and a bit grassy, and filled with beech trees. These high, windy gaps must be perfectly suited for these trees because virtually every southern Appalachian ridge in the 5,000' elevation range has them. There are high gaps named Beech Gap all over the southern mountains from Virginia to Georgia.

Those are the kinds of names that have character – local, rural character: Beech Gap, Balsam Mountain, Laurel Top, Snake Den Trail, Rocky Top. They have a primitive, regional flavor that is missing from names like Mt. Le Conte or Mt. Cammerer. Names like Devils Den, The Boulevard, or Spence Field aren't quite as natural, but they are colorful and folksy. Names like Clingman or Guyot are just bland. Those mountain tops named after famous scientists and explorers got their names when they were mapped and measured in the mid-1800s. These explorers tended to name these prominent peaks after themselves and their friends, rather than the names given them by the Cherokee and the local white settlers. Some guys never even hiked up the mountains that are named after them. Granted, many major peaks had several names, so the geographers did impose some consistency, and some of the names do honor men who are worthy of being remembered, but those names diluted the earthy, local character that pervaded the topography. White Rock, Big Balsam, and Smoky Dome became Mt. Cammerer, Mt. Le Conte, and Clingmans Dome.

The town I live in used to be called Mossy Creek, but now it's called Jefferson City. Now I like Thomas Jefferson as much as the next guy, but Mossy Creek has *character* – a rural charm that Jefferson City just doesn't have, which is exactly why the city fathers 100 years ago changed the name. They were embarrassed by the parochial name. Likewise, the college where I teach was once the Wampus Cats. Today we are the Eagles. Same motives, same process – local *character* assassination.

A later nomenclature commission finished the job with names like Charlies Bunion and Mt. Kephart. I'm thankful that the explorers and committees didn't have more friends; otherwise, we'd have no Eagle Rocks, Defeat Ridges, Maggot Ridges, or Deer Creeks left. They'd all be named Smith River or Jones Peak.

Harvey Broome in *Out Under the Sky of the Great Smokies* suggested that we not even name mountains and rivers because people would be less likely to go to places that had no names. Planes and trains couldn't run without named destinations. Erasing all the names could solve the problem of over-visitation of our national parks. He extended the logic, saying that war would be impossible because people could not fight a country which they could not name. Might be worth a try. Or, just keep the old, local names. Would anyone really fight over a spot called Maggot Ridge, Huggins Hell, Devils Den, or Bone Valley?

The three of us reconvened at TriCorner Knob (a pretty good name, although I've heard better), the halfway point on our trip, around noon, seven hours after the start. This was one of those places where Greg and Keith had to wait 10 minutes for me to catch up so we could fill our water bottles. I, the weak link in the chain, was ensuring that we didn't make good progress. Greg and Keith's fast pace wasn't helping us to get finished faster. It simply meant that they got to rest longer on our rest stops. It probably frustrated them, but it's their own fault for having a hiking partner who's 10 to 15 years their senior.

At TriCorner Knob we spent some time doing sock adjustments and foot repair. We cut moleskin and stuck it to every red or sore spot possible. Uphill hiking is tough on legs and lungs. Downhill hiking brutalizes legs and feet, especially toes. Since there were plenty of ups and downs, we were getting a nice variety of blisters and bruises. Blisters on our heels. Blisters between our toes. Bruises on the top of our feet. Sore knees, both front and back. Even our toenails ached. It would have been nice to relax at these occasional stops, but they were more like NASCAR pit stops than rest stops. We'd spend the entire time patching, pulling, rearranging, readjusting, and refueling. We also did some math…

As we sat at TriCorner Knob for a few minutes, we did some quick and easy calculations which told us that we were making a little better than 2 mph. We clearly would be hiking after sunset. Once that became clear, then we began doing a little more math, and it began to reveal an option that we hadn't seriously thought about before: where would we be at sunset? Our calculations told us that we had a pretty good chance of being on top of Mt. Cammerer – one of our favorite places on the planet – as the sun set. That would be too good to be true, spending sunrise on Charlies Bunion and sunset on Mt. Cammerer – two of the best grandstand views in the eastern half of the park.

Then we began to consider how hard this was going to be – the pace and the timing. We wondered aloud how many others had ever seen the sunrise from Charlies Bunion and the sunset from Cammerer on the same day. At first we figured the number to be in the hundreds, then as we thought about hiking in the dark at both the beginning and the end, we talked ourselves down into the dozens. Then we began to wonder if anyone had ever done it. We hadn't embarked upon this trip to be the first people to do anything, and we couldn't believe (and still don't) that we could be the first to do this. There have been just too many hikers and too many years for there to be any significant "firsts" left to do. On the other hand, we've never heard of anyone doing this particular combination. At the very least, membership in the club must be quite small, and we were hoping to be inducted that evening.

So, today would be like many other days spent outdoors – racing the sun. We had been hoping to finish by sunset, so we had been hiking vigorously. At TriCorner Knob we discovered that we were losing that race – we'd be hiking a few hours in the dark. So, the race was off. We could relax... until we decided to aim for sunset on Mt. Cammerer. The race – and the pressure to win – was on again. It seems that hiking should be free and unhindered, yet it rarely is. There's almost always a destination to reach and a schedule to keep. It's often the tyranny of the deadlines and responsibilities of our civilized life, but sometimes the deadline is sunset. You must get to the next shelter or the next campsite or the car or something before dusk. So we hurried, hiking as fast as the weak link, the old mule, would allow. But somehow, in this section, I didn't lag too far behind, and we made pretty good time. We covered 10.5 miles in about 4¼ hours. That's pretty close to 2½ mph. Not bad after having already hiked 15 miles.

But it was a tough, tough stretch. The terrain was no better and no worse than the previous 15 miles, but that extra half a mile per hour really took its toll on us. Going up and down and up again and down again at a faster than comfortable pace without any significant breaks for over 10 miles was grueling. We were definitely in the "gotta get there" mode, which is not normally a good mode for hiking. It can suck the joy out of a hike pretty quickly.

But the rush paid off. Keith and Greg arrived at the Cammerer lookout tower about 10 minutes before I did. They heaved themselves up the final few feet of rocky ledges and into the rustic, rock-and-wood firetower. (There's a sign next to it explaining that this is a "lookout" not a "tower." Okay, whatever.) They were shouting at me to hurry, and I got to the tower just as the sun began to sink behind the distant ridges. Pictures were snapped. Kudos were expressed. Feet were sore.

Legs were stiff. We sat in the old CCC rock and wood lookout for 15 minutes, trying to recuperate.

As we sat there, Greg muttered, "Boys, I just spent my last nickel."

Well said. "Spent" was the perfect word. We were spent like mayflies after mating, quivering and dying after the experience of a lifetime, thinking, "Yeah, it was worth it."

Our problem was not only that we were completely spent, ready to quiver and die after a mountaintop experience, but that we still had five miles to go. The fact that the sun had just sunk over the horizon didn't help the situation. This was the downside to being on Mt. Cammerer at sunset. We'd be hiking down to the car in the dark, and the moon would not rise to shed its light for another four or five hours. We didn't know it at the time, but we would soon discover that the trail would be ankle deep in oak leaves, hiding the rocks and roots in the trail and making for treacherous walking. A sprained ankle just waiting to happen.

As darkness fell we backtracked 0.6 miles back to the AT, adding 1.2 miles to our 31.4 AT miles. We began an immediate descent. We had started the day at about 5,000' and we presently were at about 5,000'. Our total ascents for the day had been about 6,000', and our total descents were about 6,000' as well. We would now descend a final 3,000' in 5.2 miles, in the dark, in ankle-deep leaves, on sore feet, using tired legs and flashlights. The hike didn't go well. Or, actually, it went as well as it possibly could, considering the circumstances. Amazingly, we had no mishaps, no twists or breaks, but the hike was painful drudgery, and I was nearly lame by the end. The backs of my knees – hamstring tendons connecting calf with thigh – were hurting fiercely. I know it's common to say "I couldn't have walked another step" at the end of a tiring hike, but honestly, if the hike had been another mile, I would have been crawling on hands and knees.

At 8:15 pm Greg and Keith arrived at the car they had left in Davenport Gap about 24 hours earlier. I came limping in about 30 minutes later. Normally, that would mean that I had been about a mile behind them, but in this case I was moving so slowly that it was probably more like 100 yards. For the first half of the trip, I stayed motivated and moving from the combination of peer pressure, testosterone, and carbohydrates, but those had all evaporated into thin air several hours ago. Now for this last leg the only thing that kept me going was a lack of alternatives. I kept hiking down that ridge because I *had to* keep hiking down that ridge. There was no other choice. So I just kept walking. It took me almost 3 hours to hike down that final 5.2 miles – about 1.75 mph. I bet the last mile was about 1 mph, and the last tenth of a mile was almost stationary.

At Davenport Gap we snapped a couple of pictures, got in the car, and drove toward Big Creek and I-40. The ride home after a good hiking, camping, or fishing trip is often uneventful, even subdued. There's not usually as much talking as you might expect because you're tired, and there's nothing left to say. About all we could manage was, "Can you believe it?" Or, "Yeah, that was amazing." Pretty primitive conversation, actually. You'd think three educated friends could come up with something more stimulating and thoughtful, but we couldn't. We'd just gotten thrashed and were still licking our wounds, so about all we could do was re-state the obvious in four-word sentences.

That night when I got back home, I plopped down in a soft chair, numb and wondering where I belonged. For those 15+ hours we had been totally immersed in the great outdoors. Sitting at home that night after the hike, I was in an alien land. "What am I doing sitting in this chair, indoors? I don't belong here. I should be outside walking." It's like stepping out of the theatre after an intensely captivating movie. When you re-enter the real world you are temporarily disoriented, and it takes a few moments to figure out where you are and what year it is. It's undoubtedly the same feeling a fish has when it's out of water.

When it's all said and done, our day had been the hiking equivalent of a hurricane. The rush of trees, rocks, wind, sun – it was all a blur. We were battered and bruised and a bit numb, and we felt lucky to have survived. It was one of those experiences that you'd like to tell your friends and co-workers about, but you quickly realize that they just don't get it. Someone at work asks what you did yesterday, and you tell them that you had a great 33 mile hike in the mountains. Their response is, "Wow, are you serious? That's a long way!" Then the microwave beeps, and they walk away to get their soup. Thud. End of conversation.

The next day Greg Harrell emailed some pictures to me. One showed me standing in Davenport Gap next to one of those brown trail signs with white lettering. It said: *Newfound Gap 31.4 mi.* I had a look of resignation and disgust on my face, not the expression I would normally wear after a fine Smokies hike. You know how you'll do something challenging, and it's not fun while you're doing it, but it becomes fun a few days later? Well it's been several weeks since we did our marathon hike, and I'm still waiting.... I have fond memories of the first ten hours; the last five hours, not so much. In fact, I have very few memories at all of those last few hours, sort of like people who are abducted by aliens and can't account for those missing hours, but their new bumps and bruises lead them to suspect that something unpleasant has happened.

Would I do it again? Yes. It's as crazy a stunt as a middle aged guy can do without getting in trouble with his wife or the law. That alone is reason enough to do this trip. *Could* I do it again? I don't know. This may have been my first and last marathon day hike. I may have just slipped in under the wire, before this aging body puts a stop to such foolishness. As Keith says, "Your only problem is you've had too many birthdays." Yeah, I've got to stop that.

Greg and Keith are already talking about doing the western half (41 miles or 33 miles, depending on the starting point). I'm seriously considering declining the offer. Honestly, I'd be doing it just to say I did it, and not because I really *want* to. And to be honest, I'm not sure I'm physically up to the challenge. But to sweeten the deal, Keith had an interesting suggestion – reverse everything and hike mostly at night under a full moon. We could hike a couple of hours in the late afternoon, then be somewhere dramatic when the sun sets and the moon rises. Then we'd walk all night and be somewhere dramatic for the sunrise. Then we could walk the final few miles in the morning light. Interesting plan, but it doesn't change the fact that I've had about a dozen more birthdays than they have.

By the way, you probably noticed that "it" never happened – no broken bones or lost equipment. Of course, there were aching muscles and joints and burning blisters, but that's normal and expected. The weather was perfect. We had the right equipment. Our feeble bodies (barely) passed the test. Unlike most excursions, nothing – absolutely nothing! – went wrong. That's rare, really rare.

I dread the day that our dues for this trip get paid. It won't be a pretty sight.

Chapter 7
Out Under the Moon of the
Great Smokies

Camping in the Smokies in the dead of winter is rarely dangerous but always uncomfortable, especially at night. For instance, the decision on whether or not to get out of your sleeping bag to pee is a dilemma not easily resolved. Like wars in the Middle East and budget cuts, there are no good options. Do you try to ride it out until morning, or do you get up and walk out into the cold night and get it over with so you can sleep with peace of mind and bladder? And what if the urge strikes twice in one night? Three times? For men of a certain age, a supply of FloMax can be more important than wool socks and a warm sleeping bag.

One factor in favor of getting up is the beauty and quiet of the night, especially if you are at an open, high elevation shelter or campsite. As you stand out in the open on a cold, cloudless night, the stars will blaze more clearly than you've ever seen before. While you can't quite reach up and touch them, the stars and moon do seem so close that you could probably hit one with a rock. You'll stand there wondering why you don't do this more often. Then your feet begin to get numb, a frigid breeze kicks up, you begin to shiver, and you remember why you don't do this more often: it's hard. Just as you've got to be in the right frame of mind to appreciate the cold, you've got to have the right frame of mind to fully appreciate the night. To appreciate them both simultaneously isn't quite super-human, but it does seem to be beyond the grasp of most of us most of the time, including me now that I'm not as young as I used to be. In recent years, I've spent more days but fewer nights in the Smokies. Now the nights are usually brief, beautiful, warm weather walks.

The walk from the Clingmans Dome parking lot to the observation tower at the top takes about 20 minutes. Some publications call this half-mile walk "strenuous," probably because it's steep and steady. However, it doesn't feel strenuous to me because it's short, it's paved, and there are wooden benches along the way. Although most Smokies visitors rarely venture far from their cars, Clingmans Dome is an exception. Throngs of normally sedentary people make the walk up to the concrete observation tower at the top of Clingmans. Being one of the most heavily-visited sites in the park means that parking is a problem, crowds are a problem, everything is a problem. Except at night.

On an April evening soon after the road to Clingmans Dome had re-opened for the season, I drove up through Pigeon Forge and Gatlinburg to Newfound Gap with only a minimum amount of traffic hassle. It was still the off-season, it was a weekday, and it was almost dark, so traffic was light. It was one of those drives so common to the Smokies – you drive along, glad that the weather is clear and clean, and then you encounter patches of fog along Clingmans Dome Road. By the time you reach the top, you are engulfed in clouds, wondering where they were 30 minutes ago. Then you realize that 30 minutes ago they were probably right here. You are the one who was absent. You were several thousand feet lower, below these clouds that seem to cling to Clingmans Dome in all but the coldest weather. *Cling* to *Cling*mans. It seems like there ought to be a story explaining that coincidence, but there's not. It's just a coincidence. The guy's name was Clingman.

And, of course, it was windy. Windy on the road, windy at the parking lot, windy on the trail, and windy at the top. The wind can change a peaceful night into an intimidating, unfriendly event. If I really believed in Mother Nature as a real, personal force, I'd say she was angry. A lonely, windy night can make you believe things like that. It feels like the malevolent spirit of the mountain means you harm but is playful enough to warn you before killing you, like a backyard cat playing with a soon-to-be-dead mouse. You begin to wonder if maybe all those frail tourists in their motel rooms aren't frail after all. Maybe they have good judgment.

So, it was April, it was cold, dark, and windy, and I had the mountain all to myself. The walk up to the top was uneventful, as a walk on pavement usually is. It's a different hike than it was 30 years ago. Back then it was shady and enclosed by the spruce-fir forest. Today, it is much more open as the large fir trees have been exterminated by an invading, exotic insect – the balsam wooly adelgid. The extent of the plague won't be quite as thorough as the chestnut blight. Most firs are able to live for 5 or 10 years before they succumb. But they do succumb. All of them. Their skeletons stick out of the young forest like silver telephone poles, and we now speak of the mature fir forest in the past tense: "The spruce-fir forest *was....* The fir trees *were....* The walk to the top of Clingmans Dome *used to be....*"

At the top of the mountain, the spiraling, concrete tower seems out of place. It looks like it came out of the same mind that gave us aluminum Christmas trees, cars with huge tail fins, and abstract art. I suppose the concrete and the ramp are made to accommodate the heavy foot traffic of the thousands of visitors, but tonight there is only a single pair of feet, and I feel a bit pleased with myself for having outsmarted the crowds.

The wind continued to hurl the clouds over the top of the mountain. As I stood at the top of the tower with my face to the wind, a mass of clouds blasted toward me and pushed me backwards a few feet. It wasn't the strength of the wind. It was the sudden burst of clouds racing toward me out of the darkness that startled me. One moment I was looking into darkness, the next moment a formless mass came barreling toward me out of the dark. I instinctively stepped back the way you'd step back if someone suddenly and without provocation threw a punch at you.

Through the occasional breaks in the clouds I was reminded of why there are better places than Clingmans Dome to visit at night. The reason is Pigeon Forge, or more precisely, the lights of Pigeon Forge. They have a beauty of sorts to them, a *civilized* beauty, but from the top of Clingmans Dome at night it's too much of a good thing. The lights of Pigeon Forge and its northern neighbor Sevierville are out of place in the darkness of the mountains. Civilization – whether in the form of traffic, politics, TV, or streetlights – is like fertilizer. A little bit can be good for you, but too much will kill you, withering your body and finally your spirit – and it may be more than just a coincidence that manure is a common fertilizer. The Pigeon Forge and Sevierville conglomeration is just too much for me – driving in it during the day and seeing it from a distance at night.

There's another problem with Clingmans Dome. During the peak visitation months of summer, the views are somewhere between mediocre and lousy because of humidity and pollution. You might think that visiting Clingmans Dome at night would help because of the cooler temperatures, but it has been my experience that a hazy day will in a few hours become a hazy night. As you stand on top of Clingmans you sense that you are in a bowl of haze – a bowl with an open top. The only decent summer view, even at night, is straight up.

If you can visit on a cold day in early April or, better yet, in the dry season of November, then you will probably have good, crisp views and few people. Those are the best days to visit Clingmans, day or night.

Of course, the views are even better from December through March, but during those months, you have to really, really want to see the view from Clingmans because the road is closed. You'll have a 14 mile round trip walk. Now I'm not opposed to a 14 mile day hike in cold weather. It can be a fine experience, especially on one of those days when the sky is a deep, deep blue and you can see forever, but on a cloudy, snowy day you'd be better off hiking elsewhere. Save the Clingmans hike for a clear day since the whole point is the 360° view from the top.

So, a night-time visit to Clingmans Dome is interesting and even beautiful if you like city lights from a distance, but perhaps not the best use of time and energy unless your goal is a sense of pride from outwitting the crowds. Otherwise, there are better nocturnal options, ones with fewer lights, less pavement, and more adventure.

A night-time hike is not as foolish or unnerving as it sounds. It's not easy, mind you, but it can be safe and memorable, even magical. But the moon and weather (not to mention your job) have to align because in hiking, as in comedy, fly fishing, and love, timing is everything. The window of opportunity is only a few days or hours long. So when the window opens, you'd better jump through.

And if jumping through a window has a covert, illicit, feel to it, so much the better. You are, after all, outfoxing the crowds by visiting the park under the cover of darkness. On several occasions, when I've mentioned to someone that I was headed to the park for a night hike, their immediate response was, "Is that legal?" I'm always tempted to look both ways for snitches, lean closer to the listener, and say in a hushed but stern tone, "Hold your tongue, fool! You'll get us arrested." That's the way legends are born, and it's every outdoorsman's dream to become a legend. And, by the way, night hikes are perfectly legal.

Thursday was a muggy 80 degrees. Friday brought severe thunderstorms. Saturday would be 70 degrees and extremely windy. By Sunday and Monday there would be increasing clouds and a chance of snow flurries. So Saturday – clear, mild, but very windy – was my only chance to try an evening hike to Andrews Bald. I would walk there in the evening, watch the sunset, sit while darkness settled in, then walk back to my truck under a waxing half moon, meaning that as the sun set, the half moon would be directly overhead. If the clouds cooperated, then I'd have a bright, moonlit walk back.

After doing chores around the house for most of the day – with an eye on the sky – I drove through Pigeon Forge with only a moderate amount of traffic. There would be, I was told, a hot rod show the following Saturday; US 441 would be shut down and crowded for hours. I was glad to have dodged that bullet, but I knew that I had just used up several pounds of good luck. My account was severely overdrawn already, so I knew I'd have to pay some dues in the near future. The clouds on the far western horizon suggested that maybe I'd be struck by lightning tonight – which in my accounting scheme is a fair trade for avoiding a hot rod show in Pigeon Forge.

A sunny Saturday in mid-April should be moderately crowded in the Smoky Mountains, but since it was getting late in the day, most folks were either at the picnic areas, or in restaurants in town, or driving through Cades Cove looking for wildlife. The road leading to Andrews Bald had been roused from its winter hiatus by Mother Nature and the National Park Service. Mother Nature had melted the ice and snow while the NPS rangers had unlocked the gate on the morning of April 1, and I snuck through this window of opportunity two weeks later. In another week or two, the encroaching humidity would begin to wash out the views, so it was now or November.

At this high elevation – about 6,300' – there was still the look and feel of winter. While the lower elevations were bursting with new life, the higher elevations had not yet hit their full stride. They will have to wait a bit longer, peaking in late June with the blooming of the flame azaleas and the catawba rhododendron. Late June is a great time for this hike to Andrews Bald, but today I'm not here for the flowers; I'm here for the crisp evening views, and the waxing half moon, which will provide the light for my night hike back to my truck.

I pulled into a half-full parking lot at Clingmans Dome around 6:30pm. A few people were starting their half mile walk to the concrete observation tower at the top of Clingmans Dome. They were, I presume, planning to enjoy the 360° view, followed by a sunset, all from the highest point in the park. It's a pretty good plan for this time of year. If you are going to visit Clingmans Dome, it's best to do it in April or November. The Clingmans Dome Road is closed December through March, and it's crowded during the summer and fall; that leaves spring and November as your best chance.

Of course, none of that matters to me tonight because, like Robert Frost, I'm going to take the path less travelled, hoping it will make all the difference. So, at the start of the paved trail to the top of Clingmans, I'll veer off to the left onto Forney Ridge Trail which will take me a quick and easy 1.8 miles to Andrews Bald. I hesitate to even call it a hike. It's more of a walk, but with plenty of rocks underfoot to make my steps a bit tenuous.

Two miles is more than enough to deter virtually everyone who visits the park. This is enhanced even further by the fact that Clingmans Dome – the highest point in the park – acts as a magnet which draws most visitors to it and away from Forney Ridge Trail. Ask the typical Smokies visitor, or even locals, about Forney Ridge, and they'll have no idea where it is nor why anyone would care. It's not exactly a carefully guarded secret, but like I said, it's a 1.8 mile walk, which is about 1.75 miles too far for most folks.

I'm doing this during the off-season, but this evening hike can be done easily during the peak summer months. The parking lot will have a few people who want to watch the sunset from Clingmans Dome, but most visitors will be down in the towns eating supper. And, of course, the few people that are parked here are about to walk to Clingmans Dome, not Andrews Bald. No matter what the season, there will be very few people with you on Andrews Bald. The prospect of a return hike at night scares them away.

When I arrived, there were maybe 50 cars in the parking lot, but on my walk to Andrews I saw only five small clumps of people who had just ended their afternoon on the bald and were hiking back to the parking lot. That's five cars belonging to Andrews Bald hikers. The other 45 cars belonged to the Clingmans visitors. Yep, taking the path less travelled does make a difference.

And if that less travelled path is dark, you'll almost certainly be alone. So planning this hike to coincide with a waxing half moon is important.

A waxing half moon? If you are like most of us, you might need a little help here because you studied this stuff in your 7th grade science class, but haven't had to think about it since that final exam. In the process of conquering the darkness with fossil fuels and electricity, we have become alienated from the things that happen at night – the animals, the stars, and the phases of the moon. We just aren't outside much after sundown, and when we are, we are usually surrounded by the blinding glare of city lights. So, we've lost touch not only with the night sky but with thousands of years of human knowledge. I can't say that I frequently feel the urge to get in touch with the thousands of generations of humans that have preceded us, but it is nice to know that whenever I look up in the sky and think about the stars or moon, I'm doing exactly that.

Back to our 7th grade science lesson...the moon takes about 4 weeks to go through its entire cycle. It takes one week to go from the tiny sliver of the new moon to a half moon and another week to go from this "first" half moon to a full moon. This is its waxing (growing) phase. The third week is spent shrinking (waning) from full to half (the "second" half moon). The final week sees the moon wane further from half to new again. You probably knew all that.

But here's the part that is probably a bit fuzzy to you. The various phases of the moon will light up different segments of the night. A full moon will rise in the east at the same time that the sun sets in the west. This full moon will spend the entire night moving across the night sky and will set in the west just as the sun once again rises in the east at the beginning of the following morning. The *full* moon has enlightened the *full* night.

You might think that a night hike should take place under a full moon rather than a half or ¾ moon. Not necessarily. While a full moon on a clear night will be bright, it will also be low in the sky for the first few hours (and the last few hours) of the night. Depending on when you intend to hike, it may be better to night hike under a ¾ or ½ moon because they may be higher in the sky right after sunset. Here's how that works.

The moon rises about an hour later each night as it goes through this month long phase. This means that some weeks the moon lights up the first part of the night and other weeks the latter part of the night. A quick and easy way to remember this is to remember that the "early" (waxing, growing) moon lights up the *early* part of the night, the full moon lights up the *full* night, and the "late" (waning, shrinking) moon lights up the *late* part of the night. So, at the end of the moon's first week, the moon is half full and is going to light up half the night. Because this half moon is its first or early half, it lights up the first half of the night – from sunset to midnight. In other words, just as the sun sets, this half moon will be directly overhead and will sink over the western horizon at midnight. One week later the full moon will light the entire night. Yet another week brings another half moon – the second or late half moon. This half moon will light up the latter half of the night – from midnight to sunrise because it doesn't rise at the eastern horizon until midnight. When the sun rises about six hours later, this half moon is directly overhead.

So, if I will be night hiking in the early part of the night, maybe the first hour or two after sunset, I prefer an early (waxing) ½ or ¾ moon. The fact that it is an "early" moon means that it will light the early part of the night, starting at sunset and disappearing over the western horizon a few hours before sunrise. The fact that it is ½ or ¾ rather than full means that it will be fairly high in the sky as the sun sets.

On the other hand, if I will start hiking at 4 am or 5 am, I'll be hiking at the very end of the night, so I want to hike under the moon in the late weeks of its cycle. I'll time my hike for a ½ or ¾ waning moon, ensuring that this bright moon will still be high in the sky during those couple of hours preceding sunrise.

To make it even simpler, remember this: for a hike during the hours before sunrise, it's best to go 3 to 7 days *after* the full moon; for a hike soon after sunset, go 3 to 7 days *before* the full moon. This rule will give you a bright moon, high in the sky.

So I walked alone, with a strong, evening wind whisping through the trees. This top two miles of Forney Ridge Trail is mostly spruce and fir trees. Normally, you can tell the spruce by their pointed, stiff needles and the fir by their rounded, flexible needles. Unfortunately, there's an easier way to distinguish between the two: the big trees are spruce and the small ones are fir. The fir trees don't get big because they are all killed by the balsam adelgid once they get 10 or 15 feet tall. So anything taller than about 20 feet is almost certainly a spruce.

As I hiked to the bald and encountered the hikers heading in the opposite direction, we'd swap "howdies" and keep walking, occasionally stopping to exchange news and information. (Day hikers don't normally have as much news as overnight, long-distance hikers, but it's still common etiquette to tell them they are almost there or to ask how it was at the top.) As we'd pass on the trail about an hour before sunset, I could see the question in their eyes and expressions: "Hey, man, are you sure you know what you're doing? It's getting late, and you're heading in the wrong direction, aren't you? You're going to be out there in the dark, all alone." I can guarantee that every single person I encountered thought exactly that, not knowing that being out there in the dark, all alone, was the whole point.

A great thing about Andrews Bald is that it is still a *bald*, one of only two remaining in the park. Years ago you could enjoy Spence Field, Russell Field, or other grassy areas on the high ridges of the western half of the park. They had been maintained as mountaintop pastureland by cows grazing in the pre-park 1920s and 30s, and even as late as the 1980s they were still impressively open and grassy. However, the NPS is letting all the balds revert to their original, natural, wooded state – except Andrews and Gregory. They may not be pure, unadulterated wilderness, but they are still beautiful, unique reminders of the park's previous incarnation as a home to farm families with cattle to feed. It's the same policy that keeps Cades Cove open, grassy, and attractive or that keeps a few cabins and barns standing as a testament to the human side of the Smokies. Whatever the philosophical debates about wilderness ethics, the Smokies' two remaining grassy balds are worth a visit, and Andrews is by far the easier of the two.

I emerged from the dark woods and into the open field around 7:30, leaving plenty of time to explore. The top of Andrews Bald is a serene, grassy field with scattered patches of spruce and fir trees, flame azaleas, and rhododendron. There are numerous, faint, meandering trails leading to various rocks, high spots, or shady spots – good places to sit, eat, sleep, or all three. As I walked I paid careful attention to a few landmarks and my general direction of travel.

Over the years I've learned that I have a poor sense of direction, so I have to make a deliberate effort to pay attention at times like this. On past family vacations I could get us from Tennessee to Montana or Maine on interstates, two-lanes, and dirt roads, but if we pulled into a McDonalds, I couldn't figure out whether to turn left or right as we pulled out of the drive-thru and back onto the road. My wife or kids would have to point the way back to the interstate. So finding my way back across a grassy bald was not a foregone conclusion, especially at night. As it turned out, this was easy – Forney Ridge Trail across Andrews Bald is the deepest trail, having been worn down 6, maybe 12, inches below the grassy surface.

I explored the faint trails to enjoy the changing view into this southwestern part of the park and beyond into the Nantahala mountains. I love this part of the park – Forney Creek, High Rocks, Hazel Creek, Fontana Lake. It's a wild, isolated part of the park that almost had a paved road built through it: the Road to Nowhere. It was promised in the 1940s, partially completed in the 1960s, and finally terminated in 2010. If it had been completed I would have grieved long and deep for the loss. Generally, I think the government should keep its promises; however, in this case, the promise was so potentially useless and destructive that I just hoped and prayed that the government would promise and not deliver, and thankfully that's exactly what happened.

There are good views of Fontana Lake and the Nantahala Mountains to the south and High Rocks and Gregory Bald to the west. It was the perfect stage for a sunset; however, my moonlit hike back wasn't shaping up very well. Those clouds I had seen in the west a couple of hours earlier were now much bigger, broader, and closer. This could make for a pretty sunset, but I could see that my window of opportunity for a moonlight hike was closing fast. The moon would soon be covered with clouds.

Sunset and dusk from Andrews Bald were enchanting; although, really no more nor less dramatic than the view from dozens of other locations in the park. But that made it no less beautiful. The best part was the *shaconage* – the blue haze – that spread across the mountains. It's the kind of gradual change that could be easily overlooked, especially if you focus on the sunset in the west. Yes, sunsets are great, but sometimes it's good to look every direction *except* west. In the east you'll see the ridges go from green, to yellow, to orange, to pink, to blue, to black. The transition is so smooth that it is almost subliminal. Only afterwards, as you think about the scene, do you remember the range of colors between light and dark.

I can't remember now if the south went through the same color sequence. What I remember best about the south were the innumerable ridges of the Nantahalas and the blue tint that seemed to seep out of the landscape and into the air. As the blue tint infused the valleys, the perspective, the distance seemed to get sucked right out of the air. In the bright light of the sun, I could clearly see the distance between the ridges, but as darkness grew all those ridges just seemed to squeeze together. There was height and width, but not depth.

I must admit that these colors, tints, and distances are not the kinds of things I normally notice when I am outdoors. Only when I go out with the intention of writing about it do I make the effort of really studying the scene. Trying to convert a visual panorama into words on a page is an interesting process. It raises my level of concentration several notches, which puts me on the level of the average person on an average day. At the time it felt a little like work, but I see now that it was merely something that I'm not very good at or am just too lazy to do on a regular basis. It forced me to see, really *see*, to notice things that are always present but easily overlooked.

So I sat in the thick grass, letting the night take over. The moon was already high in the sky as the sun sank and darkness deepened. Walking around the top of Andrews Bald, I saw only a few, scattered lights, plus the glow of Bryson City to the south. To be consistent, I should whine for a few sentences about the lights of Bryson City, but I can't. I like Bryson City. It's a small, simple, working-class town with only a hint of tourist trade. It's small enough that its subtle radiance seems to emphasize the darkness that surrounds it rather than detracting from it. If everything in the distance was pitch black it would give the sense of unending barrenness. The occasional light serves as a reminder that there is a vast expanse of wilderness enclosing those few, inconsequential outposts of humanity. These outposts are so small that they are completely invisible during the daylight hours and barely noticeable at night.

There was another thing that was completely invisible at that moment: Pigeon Forge and Sevierville. Their glow was completely blocked by Clingmans Dome and the main ridge crest to the north. Having a 180° view rather than 360° is a small price to pay for eliminating their distracting glow. The top of Andrews Bald, looking south into the Nantahalas, is about as close as one can get to pure darkness in the eastern US.

An hour after sunset the full weight of the night had settled in, and the bank of clouds had moved in and blotted out the moon. My walk back would be by flashlight, not moonlight. That's the chance you take when you hike in the spring. There's less humidity now than in the summer, so the views will be more expansive, but the weather is the wild card. I suppose I should have known – spring weather being what it is – that a clear blue sky during the day was no guarantee of a clear sky in the evening. But that's okay. It's good to see the mountains in all their moods. Wind, clouds, and rain are part of the package.

My next visit to Andrews Bald will be in late June when the views will be a bit hazy, but the catawba rhododendron, mountain laurel, and flame azalea will all be vying for top honors in the annual spring floral competition. Probably another evening hike because that will be the only way to escape the teeming masses that will fill every nook and cranny from exit #407 on I-40 to Clingmans Dome parking lot.

Every nook and cranny, that is, *except* Andrews Bald and those top two miles of Forney Ridge Trail about an hour before sunset.

Chapter 8
Happy New Year

September 3 through 13, 1752 do not exist in American history. In that year, a kid born the day after September 2 was born on September 14. The most immediate reason was religious, but the ultimate reason is the rotation of the earth and the earth's movement around the sun.

In 1582 Pope Gregory's calendar experts determined that the old calendar that Julius Caesar had instituted about 1600 years earlier needed to be corrected. Because of a small discrepancy in the way leap years were calculated, the calendar was off by about 10 days. So in 1582 at the Pope's command most Catholic nations and their colonies skipped 10 days, but non-Catholic nations such as England refused to follow suit. This created a rather interesting situation for the history books. For example, Shakespeare died in England and Cervantes died in Spain on April 23, 1616. Yet, Cervantes died ten days before Shakespeare because April 23 came 10 days earlier in Catholic Spain than it did in Protestant England. It wasn't until over 150 years later that England and her colonies – which included America – adjusted their calendars by dropping 11 days in September, 1752.

The first day of spring has an astronomical definition based on the position of the earth in its trip around the sun, but for most of us the easiest way to think about it is that it's the day that the sun rises exactly in the east, sets exactly in the west, the day is exactly 12 hours long, and the night is 12 hours long. On that day it just feels like everything is where it ought to be, like everything is aligned and ready to start anew. It's probably not a coincidence that most folks engage in "spring cleaning" but not "fall cleaning." We know it won't last forever, but at that moment things are in alignment and under control, and we're ready for the next round.

Astronomers don't get much respect these days. About the only time we hear from them is the first day of each season plus an occasional eclipse, so I hate to further undermine their marginal position in our popular culture, but...

For most of us, the easiest way to think about the beginning of spring has very little to do with astronomy. Even more apparent than the 12 hour day and the sunrise in the east are the numerous signs that spring has arrived. Around here, in early March, a week or two before the astronomical first day of spring, the earliest blooming plants – daffodils and forsythia being the most visible – have begun their show. The bluebirds are taking up residence in the bluebird house that we have nailed to a maple tree in our front yard. The goldfinches that frequent our thistle feeder are beginning to change from a drab olive to those brilliant yellows and blacks. It is during those early days of March that I'll have to remove the twigs, pine needles, and leaves that the wrens have put in my boots in the garage. And in March the possums begin committing their acts of highway suicide with greater frequency. It's pure possum carnage on the roads. Sometimes entire families are wiped out by a single vehicle. So the signs of spring are everywhere – in the trees, in the sky, and on the four lane. And in the mountain streams the Quill Gordons are making their appearance.

A Quill Gordon is a mayfly that inhabits cold, fast moving rivers. They spend most of their lives (a year or two) as "nymphs" scurrying around the rocks and gravel on the bed of the rivers and creeks in the mountains. In early March, when the water temperature warms to about 50 degrees, these aquatic insects go through a quick metamorphosis in which their skin splits open and an air-breathing, winged version pops out of its old skin, swims to the surface, takes its first breath of fresh air, floats along on the surface for a few moments as it dries out, and then flies away. That is, it flies away if the trout give their permission. It's at this pop-swim-float stage that they are most vulnerable to being eaten by the rainbow, brook, and brown trout that inhabit the streams of the Smokies.

For me, spring begins when the weather warms enough to warm the water in the streams of the Smoky Mountains to awaken the Quill Gordons. It is at this moment in March that spring really begins for the Smokies fly fisherman because this Quill Gordon hatch is the first significant fly fishing event of the new season. The water has become warm enough for these mayflies to become active, which in turn activates the trout, which in turn activates the trout fishermen. The official, astronomical first day of spring will be just another day in March.

It's a truism in fly fishing that the best fishing happens in the worst weather. There are days in March when the sun is warm and the sky is a deep, deep blue with none of the haze that is so common during the hot, humid days of summer. On those days it is a pleasure to be out, wading waist deep in a Smokies stream looking for mayflies and trout. Quite often on those warm, sunny beautiful days, I find few bugs and fewer fish, but that's okay because in the spring when you say, "It's just good to be out," you might actually mean it. Later on in the season, after several fishing trips and many days of warm weather, you have to catch fish to be happy, but in those early days of spring, we are much more easily satisfied. Winter has lowered our expectations and primed our pump so the slightest glimpse of green and warmth gets our blood flowing again.

All this serves as a reminder that the astronomical definition is not the one, true, divinely inspired definition of spring. You can define it however you want, based on your interests and preferences. College students see their Spring Break as the start of spring. Farmers see the day they do their final tilling as the start of spring because that's when they've finished looking through their winter seed catalogs and must now go outside and do something. To many Americans spring begins when they can go outside in comfort, maybe to start working on that tan or to play that first game of softball or golf. To fly fishermen it's the appearance of bugs, starting with the Quill Gordons.

By all accounts, spring here in east Tennessee usually starts a week or two before the official March date that the astronomers have dictated to us, and the fact that the Quill Gordons, or the daffodils, or the barn swallows, or whatever signpost you use will come early in some years and later in other years isn't a problem, except maybe to people with obsessive-compulsive tendencies. For me, the uncertainty adds a little suspense to the story. When will the swallows return? When will the sea gulls disappear from the Tractor Supply parking lot? When will I hit my first possum of the year? While astronomical definitions of spring require only that we glance at the calendar on our wall, these down-to-earth definitions have the advantage of forcing us to go outside and look around.

Likewise, January 1 is just a day in the middle of the winter. It's not the beginning of anything. On my personal calendar, the New Year begins not on January 1, but in March when our natural world reawakens, when the earth's inhabitants – the plants and animals – make their annual comeback. Leaves bud, birds regain their color, bears exit their dens, flowers emerge from the ground, and farmers mount their tractors. It's as close to a literal resurrection as nature can produce.

That's why most ancient cultures, such as the Anasazi in Chaco Canyon and the Mississippians in Cahokia, pretty much everyone, celebrated the first day of spring. They'd have special ceremonies marking the rebirth of the new year, the start of another cycle of seasons. They'd build buildings and monuments to align with sunrise on the first day of spring. Likewise, ancient Babylon, Persia, and Medieval England started their new year in March, not January. The first day of a new year coming in January rather than March appears to have been the invention of the Romans for purely administrative purposes, thus beginning the grand tradition of poor decisions by a government bureaucracy.

So, celebrating the new year in the spring rather than the dead of winter has a long, long history. If you'll make this change in your thinking, you'll merely be doing what practically all humans have done through all of human history. (And the best part is that you can celebrate by going for a walk in pleasant weather.) Those testy Romans not only gave us those annoying Roman numerals to number our Super Bowls, they added January and February to the calendar and moved the start of the new year from March to January. Western civilization has been going down the toilet ever since.

You can still see the remnants of that change over 2,000 years later in the names of our months. I took a year of Latin in high school because I believed the propaganda from the folks who said it would help my vocabulary. It didn't – although I may not be the best test case because I didn't study very hard or learn very much. One thing I did learn was to count from one to ten. I know, that's not much for a whole year of Latin, but like I said, I wasn't highly motivated when I was 15. See if you recognize these Latin words for 7, 8, 9, and 10: Septem, Octo, Novem, Decem. Sounds like September, October, November, and December – the seventh, eighth, ninth, and tenth months. Yes, long ago December was the tenth month. Do a little backward counting and you'll see that March was the first month. Adding January and February gave us twelve months, which seems reasonable, but making them the first two months rather than the last two threw everything out of whack.

On a weekday in early March, Tim Landefeld and I drove through Townsend to the stretch of water on the Little River between the Townsend Y and Elkmont Campground. This piece of water is heavily fished, but it's still one of my favorite waters in the park. I sometimes wonder if it's not fished as heavily as one might expect. It's so easily accessible that maybe everyone assumes it to be heavily fished, so no one does – a psychological twist on Yogi Berra's restaurant: everyone *thinks* it's crowded, so no one goes there.

The general consensus is that there aren't as many fish in the Little River, but the fish are bigger, keeping in mind that "bigger" means 8 to 12 inches plus an occasional hog, rather than the usual 6 to 8 inches. This stretch of the river is full of tourists and locals in inner tubes during the hot summer months, so this section is heavily fished mainly in March, April, and May, and then again in September and October. If it were late March or April, Tim and I might drive to Elkmont Campground and then walk a mile or so up the East Prong of the Little River to get to more remote water, but since this was early March and we were feeling groggy from our winter hibernation, we fished by the road, hoping to find some fish that were unmolested by other fisherman and looking for some action. After all, it had been a long, cold winter for the trout, too.

It was an in-between day weather-wise, slightly overcast but warm, so it held the potential for some decent fishing. We brought an assortment of flies on the off chance that there would be some significant, spring insects hatching. If that were the case, the fish might key in on those particular bugs and ignore our usual generic offering of an Elk Hair Caddis or an Adams.

Tim was in his waders and in the river in pretty quickly. As is often the case, I was distracted; this time by a small, yellowish bird I had seen flitting around the edge of the woods. Some folks have compared me to an old, yard dog that spends his day weaving from one distraction to another, with no clear plan in mind. I'm certain that's not true, but even if it were, I see no shame in a stream-of-consciousness lifestyle with no clear agenda. In fact, the world might be a happier place if we'd allow our routines to be interrupted by unforeseen opportunities, such as birds or wildflowers. Not a lot would get done, but then, a lot of what gets done in life is stupid or destructive, so maybe we'd end up better off. And besides…

What was I talking about? Oh, the bird in the woods. It was probably a goldfinch or some sort of warbler not yet adorned in its full, spring regalia. I watched it for about one minute but then gave up and headed to the river.

Sometimes Tim and I fish together, he on one side and I on the other, both of us working our way upstream. Other times we leap-frog each other in 100 yard segments. Tim began taunting me, "Come on, Hoov, fish this run. Even you can catch one there. It's the best water on the river." Over the course of the day, there would be half a dozen spots on my side of the river that, in Tim's estimation, would be such good water than even I could catch a fish. I read between the lines and interpreted his ridicule as an invitation for us to fish together, so I waded across and began casting upstream, and within minutes I had proved that Tim had misjudged my ability to catch fish in the best water in the river.

This first day's fishing in spring is always frustrating because my river legs have disappeared over the winter. In October and November I could wade through the submerged, slippery rocks with a degree of clumsiness that was noticeable but not humiliating. However, for the first hour of spring's first wade, I walk like a drunk who has just stood up from the bar stool. I weave and stumble, and if I'm lucky only my arm gets wet as I reach down to steady myself. Unless I do something exceptionally stupid, drowning isn't likely because most of this activity takes place in just 2 or 3 feet of water. Saving yourself requires simply standing back up, but in those few seconds of horizontality your waders get filled with water. Did I mention that the water temperature is about 50 degrees? The next time you get in a swimming pool that seems uncomfortably cool remember that its temperature is probably 65 to 70 degrees.

This first day of the new fishing year is also a time for tying knots. A fly fisherman must constantly check his back side. If he's going to cast 20 feet in front of him, he must have 15 feet of free space behind him because a backcast requires almost as much room as a forward cast. On this first spring trip I know that in my head, but not in my heart, and I have to lose several flies on branches and weeds behind me before I begin putting my faith into practice. The result is a day spent reintroducing my fingers to Duncan Loops and Double Surgeons, names that sound like Olympic figure skating moves but are nothing more than knots tied with fairly low degrees of difficulty.

Our casting stoke returns pretty quickly, partly because casting a fly rod is not as hard as the proliferation of DVDs and casting instructors would have us believe and partly because most of our casts on Smoky Mountain streams are only ten or twenty feet long. While these short casts are not very glamorous, they must look relaxed and inviting because my friends and I have been photographed many times while fishing on the Little River. There's a long stretch of the river – all the way from Townsend to Elkmont Campground, the stretch that Tim and I were fishing today – with the road to Cades Cove right above it. During the spring and summer there's a steady flow of cars, and there are lots of small parking pullouts along the road. Most of the passengers don't even see us down in the river below, but a few do. You'll often see a guy driving a pickup truck with his wife next to him and a camper top on the back. You can see the envy in the old guy's eyes as he slows down and watches as we cast and drift, cast and drift. (I know it's envy because it is the same aching look that I have when I'm the guy in the truck.)

Sometimes a car will stop, and a woman will get out – a man would probably be embarrassed – and fire up the video camera. They seem content just to get a video of a guy in a beautiful river casting a fly rod. It's not a huge boost for my ego, after all I've seen people stop their cars to photograph possums, but on the other hand, I can think of absolutely no other activity in my life that can cause complete strangers to stop their cars, get out, and take pictures. That's the beauty of a fly rod and fly line.

I was using the smallest, most delicate rod I own, a seven foot, slow action (or, as the fly rod catalogs would say, "traditional action"), four weight. Casting this small, limber rod feels like cutting through soft butter with a warm knife, and that's important because the act of casting is a big part of fly fishing's charm. Unlike many things in life – sailing and ballroom dancing, for instance – casting a fly rod on a small, trout stream is as relaxing as it looks.

In other types of fishing, casting is just a means to an end; it's what you have to do to get your bait or lure to the fish. In fly fishing, the rhythm of the rod and the movement of the line are not just a skill but a relaxation technique. Casting a fly rod is a steady flow of shooting line out and pulling line in, repeat, repeat, repeat, ad infinitum but not ad nauseum. It really does take your mind off everything else, because you have to pay attention, not in a tiring sort of way, but in a focused way, like reading a Dan Brown novel. I don't know what I think about as I fish, but I know what I *don't* think about: the mortgage, house repairs, terrorism, committee meetings, and a thousand petty annoyances. Apparently, casting a fly rod is a pleasant distraction, and even more apparently, everyone needs a pleasant distraction every now and then.

Just like any tool, a fly rod is made for one specific purpose: to cast a weightless fly. The heavier a fly is, the more awkward and clumsy the casting becomes and the further one departs from the heart and soul of the sport. In fact, when you cast with a fly rod, you are actually casting the *line*, not the fly. With spinning gear, the line weighs nothing but the lure is heavy, and it's the weight of the lure that pulls the line out. It's the same principle as dropping an anchor or throwing a harpoon. But in fly casting, the line has weight while the lure should weigh almost nothing, so you can cast a fly line whether there's a fly on the end or not.

Large, stout rods use heavier line that can cast a weighted fly like a Beadhead Prince Nymph with ease, but casting a weighted fly with my little four weight rod would be clunky and frustrating, and thus not worth doing. So choosing my smallest, most delicate rod was actually a leap of faith on my part. It was fish with light-as-air dry flies or just sit on a rock, fly rod in hand, and watch birds while Tim caught fish with his weighted nymph. No middle ground, no compromise, no looking back. Stringing up a delicate four weight is as much of a commitment as some guys will ever make.

We picked our way up the river for about an hour, and then around 11 am we began to see a few splashes on the surface, which is very unusual in the Smokies. Actually, I guess I should say that it probably happens a lot because there are aquatic insects in the river and they do swim to the surface and fly away or are eaten, but it doesn't happen often enough, widely enough, long enough, and predictably enough for us to observe it very often. But it was happening here and now, right in front of us.

We watched carefully to see the kinds of bugs that were coming off the water, and our suspicions were confirmed. It was a mahogany-brown, fairly large mayfly. You didn't have to be an expert to know that it was a Quill Gordon hatch. This time of year in these rivers the bugs would either be caddisflies (which look nothing like a mayfly), or Blue Winged Olives (which are much smaller than Quill Gordons), or the larger, brown Quill Gordons. The process of elimination was quick and easy. A month from now it could be either Quill Gordons or Hendricksons. These two mayflies look very much alike, so if you really wanted to identify them, you'd have to count the number of tails (2 for Quill Gordon, 3 for the Hendrickson), but if the two bugs look that much alike then you could just use a brownish fly, about a size 14, because trout in these waters don't have the time or patience to count the number of tails on a mayfly. In rivers with lots of insects, lots of fishermen, and gentle currents you'd swear that's exactly what they do, but not here.

Traditionally, the fly that is tied to imitate these Quill Gordons is called... are you ready for this? Quill Gordon. Wouldn't it be great if everything in life were so easy and obvious? You probably know that life rarely works out that way, and in case you don't know, fly fishing rarely works out that way, too.

If there is a holy land of American fly fishing it's the streams of the Catskill Mountains in New York – the Beaverkill, the Willowemoc, the Neversink. The "father of American fly fishing," Theodore Gordon, fished those Catskill rivers and created this fly sometime around 1900. Both the real bug and the artificial fly are named after him.

This fly is tied using the tiny, bare stem from a peacock feather which is wrapped around the length of the hook to form the body. The wing, sticking up from the neck and split in a V, is made from a few fibers from a wood duck feather. The hackle that is wrapped around the neck of the fly is a bluish-gray rooster feather. There are slight variations to this recipe, but this is the way it's been tied for over 100 years, and there's not a bit of foam or nylon yarn on it, so it's as organic as a fly can get. If you enjoy plugging into tradition, then this fly is perfect for you. Even if you don't fly fish, you ought to go to a fly shop and buy a Quill Gordon, then stick the point of the hook in a cork from a wine bottle and display it on your mantle. While you're at it, start smoking a pipe and sipping brandy from a silver flask in front of the fireplace on cold winter evenings with a black lab curled at your feet. Elbow patches on your tweed jacket are preferred but optional.

So, the hatch was rather light and lasted a little over an hour, then the fish quit feeding on the surface because there were no more bugs to eat. It had been a delightful day. We'd caught a few fish, none larger than nine or ten inches, most only seven or eight. I can't remember for certain, but I'm pretty sure we kept fishing, prospecting good water for another hour or two. We were probably hoping for another hatch somewhere, but the chances would be very slim. Whatever had prompted the Quill Gordons to hatch here had probably prompted them to hatch within a mile above and below us, if they hatched at all. So the hatch was over everywhere we went.

The one thing that is really missing from our fishing trips to this part of the Smokies is a little mom & pop's restaurant for us to finish the day. At the Hiwassee we eat at Tony's. At the AuSable we eat at Spikes. At the Little River near Townsend we eat at…Subway. It's fine, but the atmosphere is a bit predictable. As we sat at a wooden table on the porch of Subway, enjoying the warmth of a March afternoon, I raised my paper cup of iced tea and wished Tim a "Happy New Year" and finished with a "God bless us, everyone."

The New Year had begun well, and it was a fine way to celebrate. Sure, go ahead and stand in Times Square on December 31 with thousands of other people and watch a lit ball drop, or go to the Smokies in March and watch the Quill Gordons fly. To me, the choice is obvious.

Chapter 9
Tsali's Revenge

Eighteen twenty-eight was a bad year for the Cherokee. Of course, the preceding 100 years had been lousy, but 1828 was exceptionally bad. That's the year the old Indian fighter and Indian hater Andrew Jackson was elected president of the US. For the next few years, the "great white father" would be an intolerant, abusive dad with absolutely no sympathy for his "red-skinned children." In 1828 gold was discovered in the north Georgia lands of the Cherokee, increasing the pressure by white settlers for the last remaining piece of Cherokee territory. In 1828 the state of Georgia extended the state's laws into the boundaries of Cherokee territory, thus undermining the sovereignty of the Cherokee nation. The handwriting was on the wall, and many of the Cherokee could read it and understand. Ten years later, in 1838, all but a few Cherokee would be forcibly relocated to Indian Territory.

Have you ever been fishing with a friend for several hours with nothing to show for it? You're getting skunked, and at some point one of you will lose heart and quit, but the other hangs on and keeps casting. The one who quits is simply accepting the inevitable and wants to go and eat supper. He can't understand why his partner won't admit defeat. The persistent one, on the other hand, is determined to catch a fish. "That's why we call it *fishing*, not *casting*," he says. So he keeps trying, all the while questioning the manhood of the quitter.

That's what happened to every Native American tribe from the Pequot Wars to Wounded Knee: some saw the inevitability of the approaching flood of white settlers and got out with a few dollars in their pockets; others stayed, gambling that something miraculous would happen. Of course, this being more important than a fishing trip, there were hard-feelings, mistrust, bribery, murder, betrayal, and revenge in these tribal splits. My partners and I take our fishing pretty seriously, but none of our fishing trips have gotten quite that nasty... yet.

Late October, 1838. Tsali bent over his small sharpening stone, honing the blade of his knife. His father had taken it from a dead white farmer during the war between the British and the Americans in the year that Tsali was born, 60 winters ago. Tsali's father had been born in the Nantahala mountains, in the heart of the Middle Towns region of Cherokee territory. Tsali had been born and raised in the village of Cowee at the junction of Cowee Creek and the Little Tennessee River. Nineteen winters ago the Great White Father and his army took Tsali's childhood home, forcing Tsali and his family to move a long day's walk to the north to the Nantahala River, only a few miles from its junction with the Little Tennessee River. He, his wife, and their sons lived in a log cabin on 13 acres of farmland. They spent their days tending their corn fields and apple orchards, hunting in the coves and ridges, and catching fish in the river near their village. There, near the junction of the Little Tennessee and Nantahala Rivers, Tsali intended to quietly live out the rest of his years.

For several years his family owned one of the white man's guns, but it had become old and no longer worked. Tsali could perhaps have killed enough deer and bear to trade their skins for a new gun, but Tsali had decided that the old ways were good. He would hunt as he had when he was young, as his father had taught him, with traps, blowgun and darts, and the bow and arrow. Tsali resented the white man's path and no longer wanted to be dependent upon their guns, tools, and cloth. Tsali now caught bears in strong wooden cages. He caught fish in the rivers with baskets or poison. He and his family tended their crops with sticks and stone hoes, no metal. His only possession from the white man's world was his knife.

An elder in his village had once told him to take what is good from the white man and leave what is bad. Tsali now understood that there were many things from the white man's world – guns, whiskey, money, tools, cloth, beads – that seemed good at first, but became like strong, leather straps that bound the Cherokee to the white man. To use the white man's goods was to need the white man. Tsali no longer wanted to need, or even see, the white man. Tsali refused to even use the word *Cherokee*. It was a Creek word that the white man also used, meaning "people who speak a different language." Instead, Tsali used the name that his people had used for generations: *Aniyunwiya*, meaning "the best people." It was a term of dignity and history. To use the word *Cherokee* was to speak the language of his enemies – the white man and the Creek.

Nineteen winters ago the Great White Father had signed a treaty with the leaders of the Aniyunwiya giving away the land that Tsali had spent his first 40 winters on. The rivers where he fished, the mountains where he had hunted, the lands where his father had fought and died – all this land was gone. About 50 families, including Chief Yonaguska, stayed and were given their own 640 acre farms if they would farm and improve the land and detach themselves from the Cherokee Nation. They settled mostly in Quallatown at the junction of Soco Creek and the Oconaluftee River at the base of the Shaconage mountains, the mountains of blue smoke. The Aniyunwiya called this group the Oconaluftee Aniyunwiya; the whites called them Citizen Cherokee because they were citizens of North Carolina, not the Cherokee Nation. Most of the Aniyunwiya who now lived near the Shaconage mountains had rejected the white man's path. Yonaguska had given up the white man's whiskey and had convinced his people to do the same. Yonaguska would reject the white man's Bible after reading a few chapters, saying, "It seems to be a good book. It is strange the white people are no better after having had it so long."

But eight winters ago the Great White Father had told all the Aniyunwiya that they must leave their homeland and move far to the west. He said that his white people needed the land. Tsali knew that they did not *need* the land. They *wanted* the land. They wanted the yellow metal that makes the white man crazy. The white man believed money could solve all problems. Give money to the Aniyunwiya and they will disappear like snow in the sun. The white man did not understand that the land could not be sold. It was a gift from the Great Spirit to the Aniyunwiya, and they had no right to sell the land on which they lived.

But some of the leaders of the Aniyunwiya, they called themselves the Treaty Party, believed the land could be sold. They had surrendered to the white man and were leading the nation down the white man's path, and three winters ago they sold the last of the Aniyunwiya homeland. Tsali and many others believed they deserved to die. Tsali would do the deed himself if he were still a young warrior, but he was an old man, and Major Ridge, Elias Boudinot, and their Aniyunwiya followers had taken the white man's money and moved far west to a land the white man had given them.

With no homeland left, Tsali and his family had done the only thing they knew to do. They had stayed on their small farm, living there quietly and peacefully for two winters, but now as the third winter was approaching there were rumors of soldiers....

The serenity of the crisp, cold October afternoon was disrupted by a gunshot and a woman's scream which brought the members of Tsali's family running to their temporary home, knives drawn. As they approached they found four soldiers on horses, mounted in front of their wattle and daub hut, with Tsali's wife standing by the front door, calling in her native language for her family to be careful. The soldiers pointed their guns at Tsali and his sons as they approached.

Tsali's family had hoped this day would not come. The soldiers had been capturing all the Aniyunwiya that they could find, except Yonaguska's Oconaluftee band, since early summer. Tsali and his family had done what about 500 other Aniyunwiya had done. They had abandoned their home and farm and had kept on the move in the Deep Creek, Oconaluftee, and Tuckasegee River valleys, betting that the cold weather would force the soldiers to end their raids. The largest group of these fugitives was from Euchella's band. Tsali's family sometimes encountered these brothers in their wanderings, but had not attached themselves to this group. They preferred the secrecy of hiding on their own.

"Are you Charley?" shouted the chief soldier, pointing at Tsali.

Tsali knew a little English, but chose not to let the soldiers know. He raised and spread his arms and said, "Tsali."

"Very well then. Gather your family and come with us," responded the soldier.

Tsali pretended not to understand, shrugging his shoulders and looking around.

"Damn you. Come!" the soldier shouted. Like most frontier whites who believed that God and all civilized people spoke English, the soldier believed that shouting and profanity would somehow magically make non-English speakers understand what was being said. He shouted again, "Come!"

Tsali's family stood, unmoving, glancing at one another. The lead soldier barked a command and a young soldier jumped off his horse, went into the hut for a moment and came out with a few items of clothing and pottery. He threw it on the ground in front of Tsali's wife, making motions for her to pick it up, which she did.

When the others saw the soldiers' intentions, they began gathering a few belongings together, a process that didn't take very long. Soon the soldiers were pushing and prodding the family to other nearby huts, gathering Tsali's extended family together – five men, seven women, and about that many children. After several more minutes of shouting, pushing, and leading, the group was on its way, three soldiers on horseback, Tsali's extended family on foot. After about 15 minutes on the trail along the Tuckasegee River, the fourth soldier caught up with them. In the distance, where their huts stood, Tsali saw a column of smoke rising in the sky. He wondered if his home and farm near the Nantahala, which he had not seen in five moons, had been burned as well.

They continued west on the road along the Tuckasegee River. The trip to Rattlesnake Springs in Tennessee would take several days. Aniyunwiya were accustomed to walking, but with little food and small children the trip was difficult.

The impatience of the four soldiers quickly made Tsali's heart burn. White men had disrupted Tsali's life for his entire 60 years. If there was one thing in life that Tsali could expect, it was that the white man would always be waiting in the distance or around the bend, waiting to steal, to build, to kill, They were rude, cruel, and arrogant. Tsali had met some Christian missionaries during his years at Cowee who had been different from the soldiers. Instead of being rude, cruel, and arrogant, they were kind, caring, and arrogant. Whites were always arrogant. They all thought they were superior to the Aniyunwiya, and even the kind ones treated the Aniyunwiya like children.

"We'll stop here tonight!" barked the oldest soldier as they approached a creek flowing into the river. The soldiers dismounted and stretched their arms and legs. They unrolled their blankets, tended their horses, and started a fire. That evening the soldiers ate and played cards, even gambling for a few of Tsali's possessions they had taken from his hut, but they gave no food to Tsali's family. Tsali was not surprised.

The next morning the soldiers woke the Aniyunwiya family with shouts and kicks. "If we're gonna make Tennessee by tomorrow morning, you lazy bastards have to start walking!" They threw a few biscuits at the Aniyunwiya and prodded them to begin walking. Tsali led the way as his family gathered themselves, their children, and their blankets together. Tsali's wife lingered behind, helping the youngest of the children. The youngest soldier poked her hard in the ribs with his gun barrel, causing her to curse him in her native tongue. The soldier, of course, didn't understand, but Tsali's family did. They heard her say, "If I were a man, I would take that gun and shove it up your ass!!" Tsali's son's chuckled softly at the spirit in the old matriarch. But Tsali didn't laugh. He thought about her words, "If I were a man...." Tsali was a man, yet he had done nothing.

Tsali walked and thought all day. His anger burned as he thought about his wife's words. He thought about his family, his childhood, and his people. As the sun began to drop in the sky, Tsali spoke quietly in his language to his family. "We must take a chance. Prepare to fight" was all he said.

They all continued to walk quietly for a few minutes until Tsali stumbled over a rock in the trail. As he lay there for a moment feigning injury, the soldiers came, not to help, but to shout and kick. As they centered their attention on Tsali, he shouted and his sons struck with rocks and fists. The first soldier fell with a smashed skull, the second was strangled, and the third was stabbed with a knife taken from the first soldier. Tsali's blood warmed with the fight. It had been many years since he had killed a white man, and it made him feel alive, a true Aniyunwiya. The chief soldier rode away on his horse, and Tsali never saw him again.

Now it was time for a family council to make some decisions. Killing soldiers would make the army go crazy. They would not stop until the killers and perhaps entire villages were destroyed. With the army, the punishment was always greater than the crime. So Tsali's group fled to the east, back toward their beloved Tuckasegee River and the mountains of blue smoke. After they reached the Tuckasegee, they found a few Aniyunwiya who had hidden themselves in the mountains. Tsali was able to get some food and aid from these brothers, then they moved north up the river valleys, deep into the mountains, to an overhanging rock ledge that Tsali had used for shelter on hunting trips.

And there they stayed for almost a full change of the moon. They gathered food from the mountains and sometimes snuck down to the Tuckasegee and Oconaluftee Rivers to ask help from Yonaguska's band on the Oconaluftee. They were not alone. Many Aniyunwiya had fled when the soldiers came to get them and were now hiding deep in the mountains under the leadership of Chief Euchella. Others were living with Yonaguska's band, blending in with their Oconaluftee neighbors.

So Tsali waited and he wondered how this would end. Some of Euchella's people told him that there were many soldiers looking for him, and they were beginning to make threats against Yonaguska's people. Colonel Foster, who was in charge of the manhunt, thought Yonaguska's Oconaluftee band might know where Tsali was or might even be helping him. There were rumors that the army might take the Oconaluftee band west to Rattlesnake Springs and then to Indian Territory. Tsali pondered these things in his heart. Could Tsali win this contest? Could he out wait the soldiers? Could he depend on the Oconaluftee to continue to help him?

The historical background of the Tsali story is well-known. In 1830 Congress passed (with Andrew Jackson's pressure) the Indian Removal Act that finally mandated what many southerners wanted – total removal of all the Indians of the east to Indian Territory (Oklahoma). This process was slowed in court and wasn't implemented until the spring of 1838, when soldiers moved through the (former) Cherokee territory capturing approximately 15,000 remaining Cherokee, placing them in stockades, and taking them to the Tennessee River in Tennessee (mainly Chattanooga and Cleveland), and shipping them west.

Before their removal, a couple of other significant events occurred. In 1832 the state legislature of Georgia stripped the Cherokees of their political sovereignty, prohibited tribal political meetings in Georgia, and instituted a land lottery to sell Cherokee land to white settlers. This put further pressure on the Cherokee leaders to make the best deal possible and go west. So, a few of the leaders (Major Ridge and Elias Boudinot) signed the Treaty of New Echota in 1835, selling the last of the Cherokee land to the US government for $5 million. About 2,000 to 3,000 of them left to join the approximately 6,000 to 8,000 Cherokee that had left in the previous decades and were already living in Arkansas, Texas, and Oklahoma. This left about 15,000 Cherokee living in their traditional territory that had just been sold out from under them, refusing to recognize the Treaty of New Echota, and refusing to leave. Tsali and his family were part of this group.

Tsali's story so far is a mixture of fact and reasonable conjecture. We don't know the precise details of his early life, his arrest by the soldiers, or exactly how the killing of the soldiers took place, but the story so far is probably a fair representation of what did or could have happened. According to local historian George Ellison, local legend says that their hiding place, called Tsali's Rock, was a cave or rock overhang on the Left Fork of Deep Creek, near the mouth of Keg Drive Branch on the slopes of Clingmans Dome.

There are two rather incomplete versions of the Tsali story – one comes from the Oconaluftee Cherokee as told to anthropologist James Mooney around 1890; the other comes from the report filed by the military. As you might imagine there are differences between these two versions, especially concerning his final capture and death.

According to the Cherokee's own version, the story ended something like this... Tsali's family remained hidden for about three weeks, but a trusted white friend of the Cherokee, Will Thomas, met Tsali deep in the mountains. Will Thomas is an interesting character in this drama. He was the adopted white son of Chief Yonaguska of Quallatown (today's Cherokee, NC). Thomas spent a great deal of time and energy during his life trying to help the Oconaluftee Cherokee remain in the east. Most of the land that is today the Qualla Reservation in the Smokies was purchased by the Cherokee people living there but was placed in Thomas' name as a white man who could legally own land in North Carolina. In 1868 this land was finally recognized by the Federal government as a legitimate reservation, thus ensuring the Oconaluftee Cherokee's right to stay.

Thomas told Tsali that Colonel Foster who was in charge of the hunt had agreed that the remaining fugitives hiding in the mountains would be allowed to stay with the Oconaluftee Cherokee in the Quallatown settlement, if Tsali would surrender. Tsali agreed and soon surrendered to the army at a military camp at Big Bear's farm at present-day Bryson City. In rather quick fashion he was tied to a tree and shot. The execution was performed by some of the Oconaluftee Cherokee who were forced by Colonel Foster to carry out the sentence. Tsali had died to save his people, and they would now be allowed to stay in their homeland. And so, approximately 1,000 Cherokees – about 500 legal Oconaluftee Cherokee and about 500 fugitive followers of Euchella – formed the nucleus of today's Eastern Band of the Cherokee.

Or something like that. That was the version of the Cherokee people, relayed to Mooney about 50 years after the fact. That's plenty of time for a legend to grow, and for unflattering details to be sanitized. That's not necessarily what happened in this case, but if it did, it wouldn't be the first time a legend had grown from a seed of truth.

Then there's the army's version. Colonel Foster convinced Quallatown chief Yonaguska and his adopted white son Will Thomas, who was a long time friend of the Cherokee, to help in the capture of Tsali. Apparently Foster suggested to these two men that their Oconaluftee Cherokee brothers *and* the fugitives might all be allowed to stay in the Oconaluftee area if they aided in the search for Tsali's group. This possibility also convinced Euchella (the leader of many of the fugitives in the mountains) to help in the hunt.

So a force of Quallatown Cherokee (probably including Yonaguska, Will Thomas, and Euchella) soon captured all of Tsali's group except Tsali himself. A Cherokee firing squad executed three men of Tsali's family, those thought to be primarily responsible for the killings. This manhunt had been dragging on for almost a month, so Colonel Foster declared that his role in the hunt was over and that all the remaining Cherokee in the region, both the Oconaluftee Cherokee and the fugitives who had not yet been taken to one of the temporary forts, could stay. Then Foster and his men left the area, having completed their mission of rounding up as many fugitives as possible.

A day or two after Foster's regiment left, the Quallatown Cherokee captured Tsali and brought him to Big Bear's farm. Will Thomas and Euchella had discovered the location of Tsali's refuge and led several soldiers to him. Upon his capture Tsali was tied to a tree, and shot in the same manner as the other three. The manhunt was finished. The search for fugitive Cherokees was finished. Yonaguska and Will Thomas' Oconaluftee Cherokee and the fugitive Cherokee, including Euchella's group, were allowed to stay, forming the basis of today's Eastern Band of the Cherokee on the Qualla Reservation.

Like Mooney's Cherokee version, the army's story may or may not be entirely accurate. In the army's eyes, there were bad Indians (Tsali and other fugitives) and good Indians (Yonaguska and others willing to cooperate with the army). It would be easy for the army – and maybe even the Oconaluftee Cherokee – to see the death of Tsali as simply a bad Indian killed by good Indians. End of story. If the army assumed that a "bad Indian" such as Tsali was incapable of self-sacrifice and noble intentions, it wouldn't be the first nor the last time that such assumptions were made. Decades later, this narrow view of the native people would harden into a simple adage: "the only good Indian is a dead Indian."

So if Mooney's Cherokee version is true, Tsali willingly gave up his life for his people. If the army's version is correct, Yonaguska and Euchella's Cherokee were collaborators in the capture and execution of the "bad Indian" Tsali. It was a political expediency – help the white military so they could stay in their North Carolina homeland. In either case, Tsali is a martyr of sorts, but in Mooney's version, the Quallatown Cherokee come out squeaky clean. In the military's version, not so much.

The truth perhaps lies somewhere in between these two versions. Or, as they say in the movies, the story you've just been told is "based on true events." Which I take to mean that a few of the characters actually existed, but beyond that you can't necessarily believe anything you see or hear. It's an appropriately skeptical stance when watching anything from Hollywood, or when hearing an event described by people who have a dog in the fight, as both the Cherokee and the army did in 1839.

Unfortunately, turning Native Americans against each other was not uncommon in our nation's history. Usually the scenario involved the US military using traditional enemies against each other. A lot of the old Westerns hint at this when they show Indian guides traveling with the US cavalry searching for the Sioux or Apaches or whomever the enemy is in that particular movie. You can even see this in Cherokee history as they aided Andrew Jackson against their long-time enemies the Creeks in the Battle of Horseshoe Bend in 1814 in central Alabama. It was a typical case of "The enemy of my enemy is my friend." It's the same reason the US embraced Stalin as an ally during World War II. He was Hitler's (and Japan's) enemy.

It was also fairly common for some members of a tribe to turn against other members. Men who, under different circumstances, would have been brothers would be pitted against each other. The divisive factor was usually the white man. That may sound odd and rare, but it's not. When Crazy Horse was arrested in Nebraska, members of his own Sioux nation worked with the US army to capture him. When Hitler defeated France he installed a new French (Vichy) government that would be obedient to the German Nazis. In British India, there were native Indians who served in the Indian Police, helping the British to maintain order. In recent Iraq, many Sunni Muslims see the Shiite Muslims who wield most of the power as mere collaborators with the American invaders. In such settings the good or bad intentions of the conquerors become lost in the animosity that is created when the native residents are forced to make a tough choice: either make the best of a difficult situation by cooperating with the conquerors, or continue to resist them. The Oconaluftee Cherokee, not wanting to lose their North Carolina homeland, may have chosen to cooperate with the US government in capturing Tsali; although, we can't be entirely certain of the extent of their cooperation.

Heads I win, tails you lose. Playing with a stacked deck. This is the theme – gambling and losing – of Cherokee history that was replayed 30 years later west of the Mississippi with the Sioux, Cheyenne, Arapahoe, Apache, etc. No matter what choice the Native Americans made – resistance, war, appeals to the Great White Father, adopting the white man's path, fleeing further west, staying in their homeland, surrendering and going to a reservation, signing treaties, refusing to sign treaties – the result was always the same. As one Sioux chief said, "They made us many promises, more than I can remember, but they never kept but one: they promised to take our land, and they took it." Usually over a lot of dead bodies. On the Cherokees' forced migration to Indian Territory, known as the Trail of Tears, there were many dead bodies, about 4,000 to be almost precise.

I have fond memories of the town of Cherokee. It's the kind of place a kid loves – you can play miniature golf, ride go carts, pan for gold, feed a live bear in a cage, eat fast food, visit a petting zoo, and have your picture taken with a *real* Indian. As an educated adult, I'm a little less impressed than when I was 8, but I still like Cherokee. I just have to look a little more closely and carefully to find the good stuff. But I suppose that shouldn't come as a big surprise. That happens to most things in life, doesn't it? As a kid you see through a kid's eyes. In Cherokee you see bears and Indians, and it's really, really cool. At home you play baseball, play video games, play outside (back in the days when kids played outside), visit cousins, go to the mall, and spend your parents' money that, as far as you know, they pick from the money tree that grows in the back yard. It's a carefree, unthinking life with no guilt, no double standards, and no gray areas.

As an adult, life gets a bit more complicated, and you have to look at things a bit differently to find the joy and meaning. Maybe your parents had a money tree growing in the back yard, but the house you live in doesn't have one and you can't find a nursery that sells them. Half of those cousins that you used to play with have grown into fully-dysfunctional adults that you've intentionally lost contact with. The other half has intentionally lost contact with *you*. When you do go to a mall, you realize that you are about three times the age of the average mall-dweller. The world of adults is full of conflicts and contradictions with many choices being the lesser of two evils.

Well, anyway, Cherokee works like that, too. There's some good stuff there, but it's generally not the kind of thing most kids would appreciate, it's not always easy to find, nor is it spotlessly pure...

As you drive into Cherokee, you'll first and foremost be struck by the souvenir stores. Most of them sell cheap Indian trinkets, some of which are made locally and some overseas. Most of them are not authentic Cherokee, if by *authentic* you mean *traditional*.

Take the "roadside chiefs" for example.... There are several obviously full-blooded Cherokee men scattered at various spots in town who will pose with you so your wife can take your picture with a real Indian. They are usually wearing a long, feathered headdress and are standing by a tipi and a totem pole. The first problem with this is that these men are remnants of a defeated people allowing themselves to be placed on display for the benefit of their conquerors. You don't have to be a rabid liberal to see the sadness in that. I once saw a white tourist holding his young son up to one of these chiefs, saying: "Say 'how' to the injun. Say 'how, injun.'" Seeing that encounter evoked the same feelings I get when I see commercials for the Jerry Springer show – some people are treading water in the shallow end of the gene pool and should be prohibited from voting or breeding – you know, for the good of society.

Also, these roadside chiefs are costumed to fit white America's stereotype of what an Indian should be – they all live in buffalo skin tipis, carve totem poles, and wear eagle feather headdresses. None of these were part of Cherokee culture. The eagle feather headdresses were worn by the Plains Indians. The totem poles were from tribes on the Pacific coast of Canada

The tipis were not Cherokee either. They were portable homes, perfectly adapted for the nomadic lifestyle of the buffalo hunters of the Great Plains. Now this is going to disappoint you: the Cherokee (and most Native American tribes, actually) were not primarily hunters. They were small-scale farmers; what anthropologists call horticulturalists. Almost all tribes, including the Cherokee, did some hunting for meat and hides, but their primary means of subsistence was crops, such as the "three sisters" – corn, beans, and squash. And, being a farmer means that you aren't nomadic; you are settled in more permanent dwellings in small towns. In the case of the Cherokee, they lived in mud covered huts.

Their towns were scattered from the northern quarter of Georgia (including parts of South Carolina and Alabama) through east Tennessee and western North Carolina and into Kentucky, but there were three main concentrations of towns. The Lower Towns were clustered in the northernmost portion of the Georgia-South Carolina state line along the Savannah and Tugaloo Rivers. The Middle Towns were located in the southwestern corner of North Carolina in the vicinity of the Little Tennessee and Nantahala Rivers. The Overhill Towns were located just west of the Smokies along the Little Tennessee and Tellico Rivers. The location of today's reservation surrounding the town of Cherokee was occupied by a group known as the Oconaluftee Cherokee on the northeastern edge of the Middle Towns region.

So there's a lot to see in the town of Cherokee that's not an authentic part of traditional Cherokee culture. However, it's not quite that simple because sometimes *authentic* and *traditional* are not quite equivalent because another aspect of Cherokee temperament has been acceptance of the white man's ways. In other words, perhaps something can be authentically Cherokee without being traditionally Cherokee...

If you read about the Lewis and Clark Expedition up the Missouri River, you will be impressed by the fact that there was remarkably little violence and resistance by the native tribes they encountered. There were isolated events arising out of theft or misunderstandings, but almost no armed resistance by the tribes. Almost all the native tribes were a bit suspicious but were interested in establishing peaceful trading relationships with these Americans because they saw quite clearly the value of cloth, guns, and metal objects. This same general pattern held for the Cherokee. As you read Cherokee history you don't read much about battles, wars, and massacres during the early years of contact. Sustained contact with whites began in the late 1600s as white traders from Virginia and South Carolina traveled inland to Cherokee territory and developed trading posts and routes, trading deer skins for cloth, metal tools, and guns. But as trade became massive intrusion, these peaceful relations turned violent.

There were conflicts and skirmishes from roughly 1750 to 1800, as American settlers began to intrude and chip away at Cherokee land. During the 1750s and 60s most Cherokee fought against the British in the French and Indian War. They hoped a French victory would stop the flow of British settlers into the Appalachian frontier. After the French and their Indian allies were defeated by the English, Anglo-American southwestward migration increased. (Remember Daniel Boone?) During the American Revolution most of the Cherokee sided with the British. Again, it was their hope that a British victory would stop American settlers from further intrusions. You know how that turned out.

So, by the 1780s the Cherokee were 0 and 2 when getting involved with the white man's wars. Each of these defeats was followed by a flurry of treaties in which the Cherokee lost land. (It won't be a significant part of this story, but the Oconaluftee Cherokee sided with the Confederates during the Civil War, thus making their record a "perfect" 0 and 3.) During the late 1700s the Cherokee continued to lose battles and lose land, and several thousand Cherokee simply moved west to Arkansas,

Texas, and Indian Territory to get away from the wars and white pioneers and soldiers.

By 1800, with most of the traditionalists and hostiles either defeated or gone west, many of the 15,000 Cherokee who remained in the eastern homeland began pursuing the white man's path. Most were living in log cabins and were beginning to adopt the white man's tools for their farming. The Cherokee leaders created a formal government patterned on the American system of elected officials and a Congress. Many Cherokee accepted the Christian faith. Even Sequoyah's invention of a Cherokee alphabet in the early 1800s and the start of an English-Cherokee newspaper called the *Cherokee Phoenix* in 1828 were imitations of the white man's "talking papers."

In the early 1800s, many traditional Cherokee were appalled at the adoption of the white man's ways. (Tsali probably fit this description.) Such things as log cabins, metal tools, Christianity, and a written language were not *traditional*, but many Cherokee people were adopting these new ways, so in that sense these new practices were *authentic* Cherokee. Like any society, some people are more willing to adopt new ways than others. Yes, the fact that they were adopting the ways of their oppressors and conquerors gave this assimilation a traitorous flavor, but log cabins, metal tools, guns, and a written language were incredibly useful in creating a better life whether the user was English, American, or Cherokee.

This theme of assimilation and accommodation continues today in the town of Cherokee. Although I don't condone Cherokee men dressing up like stereotypical Injuns and standing by the side of the road having their pictures taken for a few dollars, they are making a living from the white tourists by providing something that they are looking for, even if it's not traditional. In other words, what makes something *authentically Cherokee*? If a Cherokee Indian rides a Harley, then what he's doing is "authentic." If a Cherokee woman and man own a nice house and two cars, then that's authentic Cherokee because Cherokee people are doing it. They are doing what many Cherokee people have been doing for 300 years, choosing some things from white American culture, rejecting others, and being

Cherokee all the while. Maybe not *traditional* Cherokee, but Cherokee nonetheless.

The chief of the Eastern Band of the Cherokee told me an interesting story several years ago. (I had a brief interview with him in his office at the Council House in Cherokee. It's a small building next to the fairgrounds. No, he wasn't wearing a loin cloth. He was in a conservative blue suit. It was just like visiting the mayor of a modest sized town.) At that time a number of native groups were protesting the use of Native American themes by professional sports teams, including a group that had recently staged a protest at an Atlanta Braves game. The chief told me that while that protest was going on near the front gate of the stadium, many of the Braves' souvenirs, such as foam tomahawks, that were being sold in the stadium were produced in a factory in Cherokee! He was less concerned about sports mascots and more concerned about providing jobs on the reservation. I'm not sure if he spoke for the majority on this issue, but it was certainly a theme that has been evident in Cherokee history and culture for over 200 years – compromise, survive, and move on; choose your battles carefully, or maybe *expediently* is the better word.

Making a buck at the expense of tradition seems to be part of human nature, at least for some people, maybe most. We see it every time a family farm is sold to a developer. There's a pretty good chance that wherever you are sitting right now was once a family home place, meaning that at some point in the past, someone chose money over family heritage. So welcome to the world of mixed emotions, hidden agendas, compromise, pragmatism, and tough choices. They all are part of that adult world we joined when we finished school, got a job, and started paying our own bills. Or, in the case of the Cherokee, when the first white trader showed up around 1700 and said, "What'll you take for that pile of deerskins?" How different Cherokee history might be if the Cherokee had responded, "Nothing, and get the hell out of my yard!"

Okay, realistically, their history wouldn't be much different, except that more of them would have died fighting in the 1700s rather than on the Trail of Tears.

So, what do I *like* about Cherokee? I like that fact that I can
go to Arby's and read the newspaper clipping on the wall about
the Cherokee High School girls basketball team winning the
state championship several years ago. I like it that one of their
stars was named Squirrel. I like the Cherokee Museum where
you can learn about Cherokee history and culture. I like the fact
that the museum's gift shop there has a lot of books and very
few cheap, non-traditional souvenirs. I like the Oconaluftee
Indian Village; although, it's set up on a heavily wooded
hillside, which is not where most Cherokee settlements would
have been. (Like most ancient horticulturalists, they preferred
the level, fertile river valleys to grow their crops.) I like to get
out of the town of Cherokee and drive around the reservation.
It's less touristy and looks a lot like any community in rural,
western North Carolina, except that you'll occasionally see a
house, church, or store with a sign written in the Cherokee
syllabary rather than English. I like the fact that the schools in
Cherokee are trying to preserve and perpetuate the Cherokee
language, but not at the expense of English. I'm glad that the
town of Cherokee provides jobs, thus reducing poverty and all
its associated ills, but I'm also glad there are some traditionalists
who want nothing to do with the town, either because it's too
crowded or because it belittles their traditional culture.

Most Cherokee people don't live in the town of Cherokee.
Most don't live on the reservation. Most don't even live in
North Carolina. They live in houses, towns, and farms in
Oklahoma, not on a reservation because there is no Cherokee
reservation in Oklahoma. They drive cars like you and me, work
at jobs like you and me, and wear the same clothes as you and
me. This strikes some people as odd, but it's really not. For
instance, some of you have Scottish roots, but you don't wear a
kilt and play the bagpipes. Those of you with English roots
don't get weepy about the Queen of England or excited about
British soccer. Most African-Americans are much more
American than African. You (actually, your recent ancestors)
assimilated and so have many of the Cherokee. Their
tumultuous and sad history makes them different from most
immigrants, but not completely different.

As white pioneers pushed south and west into Cherokee territory, some of the leaders of the Cherokee believed that their only hope of retaining their land, history, and culture was to adopt some of the white man's ways. They pursued the "white man's path," and many whites were eager for the Cherokee to become "civilized." Some of this white desire sprang from their hidden agenda to turn the Cherokee into small, individual family farmers who would mix and disappear into white rural society, in which case there would no longer be any need for the Cherokee to keep their tribe's land, because there would no longer be a distinct tribe with a need for land. They would melt into the larger, white society and their land would merge into it as well.

However, some whites genuinely wanted to help the Cherokee. The Cherokee people had experienced hunger, disease, destruction, and death during the wars of the late 1700s, and many whites believed that learning English, learning to read and write, accepting Christianity, dressing modestly, and learning to farm were the best hope for the Cherokee to survive and prosper. (It's one of life's great ironies that, given the circumstances and the flow of history, they were probably right.) So, the US government sent agents to live among the Cherokee to encourage them to adopt white "civilized" life. They distributed plows to men, spinning wheels and looms to women, and hired blacksmiths and millers to move into Cherokee territory.

Missionaries were also active among the Cherokee, encouraged by the US government, believing that an essential part of being civilized was being Christian and that an essential part of being Christian was being civilized in the European sense. Thus, both church and government tended to mix together both Christianity and white, European culture into a single concept. It was a clear example of the "White Man's Burden" one hundred years before Rudyard Kipling wrote his poem by that name. Indeed, while white Americans were "civilizing the savages" on their own frontier, Kipling's Britain was doing the same in India and Africa. Of course, an essential part of bringing Christianity and Civilization to the natives was taking their land. Even those of us with only a modest degree of insight can see an ugly pattern there.

The schools (both church and government sponsored) were seen by white society as especially important elements in the civilizing process. If the children could be educated and converted, then the next generation would be civilized after the present, traditional generation died off. Thus, boarding schools were an important agent in the assimilation of both Cherokees and all other Indian tribes. These boarding schools existed well into the 1900s. In fact, a few still exist around the US on or near Indian reservations. You can still find a few old timers who remember being sent to the boarding school in the town of Cherokee.

These kids were taught that they were Americans, not Cherokee. They were not allowed to speak their native language; they were to speak only English. They were required to dress and act as civilized Americans. The boys learned to plow and build fences (for the small, private farms they would one day own). The girls were taught to sew and cook. The longer kids lived at these schools, the less time they spent among their families and other traditional Cherokee. They began to accept the teachers' standards of behavior, beliefs, and values. In the words of Pink Floyd, they were becoming "just another brick in the wall." It's a good reminder that education is more than simply learning to read and write; it also involves learning a particular version of history and its heroes, as well as a sense of belonging to a group or a nation. Our educational system still does that today; although, we aren't suspicious of it because we weren't recently dragged out of a different culture and thrust into a totally new way of looking at things. There just aren't many savages to civilize anymore.

It's interesting that many Native Americans who attended these schools around the US have (mostly) fond memories of them. Yes, they now recognize that part of the hidden agenda was to extinguish their native culture. However, most of the graduates of these schools speak of the kind, caring teachers. They speak fondly of their friends. They were well-fed and cared for. And, they are thankful for the education they received – thankful that they were forced to learn English because it's an essential skill to success and prosperity in America. In short, they recognize that some good came from these schools, even though the schools were one step in the destruction of traditional, Native American culture. Another one of those annoying paradoxes of modern life.

It's probably safe to say that in the 1820s, no Cherokees wanted to completely eliminate their traditional culture; however, beyond that viewpoint there was a wide range of opinions toward the efforts of the US government to civilize them. Some Cherokees approved of some aspects of the civilization program – education, trading, farming, clothing, even religion. Many of the mixed-blood and wealthy Cherokee took this view because adopting the white lifestyle had been profitable for them. For example, John Ross was a mixed-blood Cherokee who owned a plantation on the Coosa River near Rome in north Georgia. He and his family lived in a two-story wooden home with glass windows, nice furniture, and fireplaces. He owned several black slaves who tended his corn, wheat, cotton, and fruit orchards. Ross was the Principal Chief of the Cherokee during their final days in the east. He had adopted many of the whites' ways, yet he was a strong opponent of the removal of the Cherokee to Indian Territory.

On the other end of the spectrum, there were traditionalists who wanted nothing to do with the white man's culture. They wanted to live their lives in their traditional land, unmolested from the white world. This group consisted mostly of Cherokee who had not benefited from the white man's life. They were mostly poor and isolated, many not even speaking English. Both Tsali and Yonaguska were part of this group. They wanted nothing to do with the white man's alcohol, religion, or language. They were against removal to the west, claiming that the Cherokee could be happy only in their traditional homeland.

And so, by 1838 when the soldiers began herding the eastern Cherokee into camps to move them west, none of the 15,000 Cherokee wanted to move west. Those that were willing to move west had already moved. We saw from Tsali's story that about 1,000 of these eastern Cherokee were able to stay, about 11,000 made it to Oklahoma, and about 4,000 died en route. A few, like Tsali, died for refusing to go. I wonder how many confrontations like Tsali's happened but never made it into Cherokee legend or military reports.

It's interesting that the Cherokee have a casino on their reservation because they have a long history of losing their bets. They picked the losing side over and over again. In the French and Indian War of the 1760s, they fought against the British, and lost. In the American Revolution they sided with the British, and lost. After the American Revolution, they fought the tide of settlers, and lost. In the 1800s many of them bet on "the white man's path" as a way to keep their eastern homeland. The white man's path led them to Oklahoma or the grave. Some Cherokee left their eastern homeland in the early 1800s before the Trail of Tears because they wanted to get away from the white man. They went west – far west – so that they would forever be rid of the white man. Most of them ended up as far west as Texas, Oklahoma, and Arkansas. Not far enough. A few ignored the white man and just tried to live their lives with their families in the rugged backcountry of the southern Appalachians. Ask Tsali and his family how well that gamble worked.

As I walked through Harrah's Casino in Cherokee, the biggest money-maker on the Qualla Reservation, I saw lots of people having fun throwing away their money. Personally, I like a good game of poker now and then, so I'm not morally opposed to a little friendly gambling, but it seems to me that a guy ought to think twice before walking into a nice, elegant casino. Just stop and ask yourself one question: where do the owners get the money to pay for all this nice lighting, carpet, and amenities? The answer should be obvious.

The next question follows logically from the first: am I going to enjoy losing my money? In the casino parking lot I saw cars and tour busses from all over the eastern US. Apparently, there are tour groups that skip America's scenic wonders and just travel around from casino to casino for the sheer entertainment of gambling. Presumably, they walk in, gamble, lose their money, and walk out happy because the point of gambling isn't to win money, it's to gamble.

If you enter the casino for the purpose of making money, you should turn around and walk away, and don't look back. Or, go to the main desk and pick up a job application because the only people who consistently make money in a casino are the owners and their employees.

I guess this would be the place where I should philosophize on people's need to gamble. Is it an inherent part of a modern society that has become wealthy and bored, sort of like juvenile delinquency? Are we so bored as a people that we search for easy thrills by playing games of chance? Is it similar to the jaded citizens of Rome watching chariot races and gladiator fights at the circus? Is life so dull for so many that it's come to this?

Like I said, this would be the place to ask all those questions, but I won't. Instead, I'll end with an interesting fact – most of the patrons in Harrah's casino were white. Most of the cars on that day were from *off* the reservation. The very society that was powerful enough to crush the Cherokee has evolved into a society that has spawned a class of people who thrive on losing their money at casinos on Native American reservations. As today's Cherokee are laughing all the way to the bank, maybe Tsali is laughing in his grave.

You've heard of Montezuma, the Aztec chief, who was killed by the Spanish conquistador, Cortez, in Mexico 500 years ago. Today, when whites go to Mexico and drink the water, Montezuma gets his revenge a few hours later. I think Tsali has worked out a similar arrangement in the afterlife. When a white walks into the Cherokee casino, Tsali get his revenge soon thereafter, at the blackjack table and the slot machines. Perhaps the casino should change its name to Tsali's Revenge.

Sometimes there *is* justice in the world, even if it takes 200 years.

Chapter 10
A Day in the Middle of Everything

Someone will occasionally ask, "How's the fishing up there in the mountains?" I suppose that could mean just about anything, but nine times out of ten it means, "Are the fish big, are there lots of them, and are they easy to catch?" At least, I assume that's what the guy means because that's what I mean when I ask that same question. Although, for some folks, if the answer to the first part of the question is "no" then they lose interest in the answers to the other two.

My usual answer is somewhat vague simply because fishing is an unpredictable venture. Just because the fish were easy to catch yesterday doesn't mean they'll be easy today. Or, just because *you* can catch them doesn't mean that *I* can. There's just not much about fishing that can be said with confidence, except that not much can be said with confidence, and I'm not even sure about *that*.

I'm not opposed to outright lying about my favorite fishing spots because fishing is important enough to lie about but not so important that I feel guilty for doing it. But because I do have a few ethical standards, I prefer to tell the truth – but in way that distorts the truth. It's a skill highly valued among fishermen and politicians. So I'll tell them that the fish are sometimes, but not always, cooperative. I'll mention that the water is a bit acidic which is not conducive to aquatic life, which includes insects and the fish that feed on them. So the fish aren't big, and they aren't plentiful. Then I'll mention peripheral details such as the beauty of the mountains or the joy of solitude, and then (again) the small fish. I don't explicitly discourage people from fishing in the park, but I do try to phrase my answer in such a way that the small size of the fish is mentioned several times. If I'll mention the small fish in an apologetic tone and then brag on the scenery, all in the same breath, most guys will stop listening, smile politely, and silently mark the Smokies off their list, which means that my rivers will be less crowded. If I ever find myself unemployed, I could probably find work as the Minister of Propaganda for some Third World dictator.

In all honesty, probably the best answer to a question about the fishing in the Smokies would be another question: "How far are you willing to walk?" Wetting a hook near Elkmont or Smokemont or near a parking area at a trailhead will probably end in frustration, but walking several miles to the middle of nowhere, away from everything, tips the odds in your favor. In this respect, fishing is like most other activities in life – the harder you are willing to work, the better the results; although, there are no guarantees which, again, is a lot like life.

I saw the truth of this "hard work/better results" axiom not long ago on the Middle Prong of the Little Pigeon River in the Greenbrier area of the Smokies. I parked my truck at the Ramsey Cascades trailhead, walked about 45 minutes up the trail, waded across the Middle Prong, and walked about half a mile upstream on an old, barely-visible trail.

Using this old path was supposed to be quicker and easier than wading upstream, but as is often the case, there is no "quicker and easier" out in the middle of nowhere. I had underestimated the extent to which this route would be covered in Stinging Nettle (aka Wood Nettle), and I soon found myself in the middle of several acres of this odd plant, with no hope of escape. I had only been here once before, and it had been in March, before the plant life explodes from the rocky soil of the Smokies. It was now late June, I was wearing shorts, and the Stinging Nettle had made its annual appearance with a vengeance.

I don't know much about the biology of Stinging Nettle. All I know is that this waist-high, summer plant has tiny hairs or thorns or something that specializes in itching. They don't dig and scratch like real thorns, but calling these little weapons "hairs" doesn't do them justice. Whatever you want to call them, they rub some sort of toxin (a mix of acid and ammonia, I'm told) on your bare skin. On this particular day, I discovered that it's not the kind of itching that you can ignore through sheer will power. It's the kind of itching that demands to be scratched, yet can't be relieved by scratching. If you've ever worked with rolls of pink insulation for your home, you know what Stinging Nettle feels like.

We've all heard the horror stories about Poison Ivy, but I've never heard any about Stinging Nettle. I'm not allergic to Poison Ivy, so I can't tell you from experience which one is worse. However, I'm fairly confident that Poison Ivy is the nastier of the two, at least in the long run. For the most part, Stinging Nettle is intensely annoying for several minutes, not several days. The only good thing about Stinging Nettle is that you know almost immediately that you've waded into it because the itching starts quickly, so you can stop, look at the plant, and tell yourself to avoid it – unless you have stupidly waded into a field of it while wearing shorts. Poison Ivy is much more insidious, almost subliminal. It's like the difference between regular TV commercials and subliminal advertising that's inserted into movies. When the TV commercials come on, you can put up your mental defenses and refuse to be fooled by the advertisers' claims, but when you've been exposed to subliminal advertising, you wake up the next morning with an overwhelming urge to buy a new car.

Luckily, I discovered that wet wading waist deep in a cold, mountain river is the perfect cure for Stinging Nettle. I don't know if the moving water washed the poison away or if the cold simply made my legs numb, like a local anesthetic. Either way, spending a few minutes in the river fixed the problem, which shouldn't have surprised me; wading and fishing in a remote Smokies river is the cure for many maladies, both physical and emotional. At that moment, calling the river "healing waters" would have been more than just poetry.

As I stepped into the river and looked around, I could tell that this place rarely sees a human being. There was no bare path along the side of the river and no worn spots on the obvious passageways over rocks and logs. The other clue was that there were fish in all the obvious spots in the river.

My usual routine is to wade my way upstream, casting to moving water in the numerous pools and chutes in front of me.

On a day when the fish are being especially gullible, I'll get a strike or a tug in most spots where a fish should be. These are those moments when a guy like me could begin to feel a bit smug, thinking that, yes, I really do know how to fly fish. Of course, a moment's reflection would remind me of all those days when I've done exactly the same thing (same flies, same tactics, same rivers), and ended the day with no fish, no strikes, no tugs, and finally no self-esteem. In other words, the fish are in charge. They are always in charge. If they decide to be vulnerable and reckless, I may catch a few. If they decide to be bored or shy, I'll get skunked. If I were a young, single guy, I'd make some sort of comparison between catching fish and meeting women. Whether vulnerable and reckless or bored and shy, either way, the women are in charge. Sometimes you catch a few, sometimes you get skunked. But since I'm not young and single, I won't venture into that long-forgotten territory.

As I've fished various rivers in the park, I've noticed a pattern. On those days when I'm catching fish easily, I'll come to a beautiful pool that has all the signs of a fish hotel. It just looks right. So, I'll cast to the obvious spots, watching and waiting for a fish to strike. Watching and waiting... and nothing happens. Those are the moments that don't make sense. The fish seem to be everywhere in the river *except* the very best spots. Then, just as I'm beginning to doubt reality and all that I thought I knew, I'll look at the river bank and see a worn spot or a small trail leading from the main trail to the riverside, and at that moment life makes sense again. This pool has been fished often by others who have either kept the fish they caught or made them so skittish that they can't be caught. These fish have been "educated," as the fly fishers say, or they've been eaten. These are the places where I'm most likely to see a rusty, illegal can of corn – a sure sign of a guy who came to catch a few fish to take home for supper. It's a pattern I've seen many times: the fish aren't where they should be, I'm momentarily baffled, then I see the worn path to the river.

It's also surprising how often the very next chute or pool up the river will have fish again, right where they should be. In other words, some folks will walk down an established trail near a river, get off the main trail and follow a small path to a nice spot on the river, catch a fish or two from that spot, then quit. They don't even bother to walk an extra twenty feet upstream or downstream to another spot to catch a few more fish. Of course, that's good news for the rest of us. Otherwise, these folks who catch a few easy fish and keep them for supper would clean out the entire river pretty quickly.

The National Park Service has for many years resisted the idea of catch-and-release regulations in the park. In other words, no fish could be kept. They all would be returned to the river. From what I understand, the NPS says that the present regulations which allow fishermen to keep any fish over 7 inches are working well. Fish populations are stable. The rivers have not been cleaned out by "meat" fishermen who keep their fish. The rivers are reasonably healthy. I suppose all of that is technically true, but I'm a bit skeptical of that logic simply because the vast majority of fisherman I've seen in the Smokies practice catch-and-release. It's rare to see a guy walking away from the river with fish on a stringer or in a creel. In other words, the rivers maintain their populations of fish because of the unofficial catch-and-release ethic that most Smokies fishermen practice. So, in a sense, yes, the present system works, but only because most fishermen follow a more restrictive, self-imposed policy. I think those occasional fishless pools are a glimpse into what would happen if more fishermen followed the official policy and kept their fish.

As you can probably tell, I release all the fish I catch in the Smokies. Shoot, I'm so morally pure when it comes to catch-and-release that I don't even take pictures of my fish for fear of stealing their souls. Of course, the fact that I don't catch large fish that are picture-worthy might have a little something to do with it, but either way, I return all my fish gently to the water. And by "gently" I mean that I use barbless hooks, I wet my hands before touching the fish, and I don't literally "throw them back." That's just a figure of speech. I'd hate to think that trout are as delicate as we seem to think they are, but it's best to play it safe and treat them like they're made of blown glass.

Catch and release is still a relatively new idea, just a few decades old. In the olden days, anyone who threw back a perfectly good fish would be put in the same category as the village idiot – worthy of pity and a source of embarrassment to the town. Stories would be whispered of why the poor soul had come to such a fate, capable enough to catch fish but not sensible enough to keep them. Today the C & R fisherman is more likely to be classified as an elitist snob, which is unfortunately sometimes the case. As I heard one C & R fisherman say, in reference to the superiority of releasing your prey, "Catch and release is what separates us from the animals." Animals don't hunt and fish for the sport; they keep their prey. Humans are the only creatures who break that law of nature. So I suppose it all comes down to this: Meat fishermen abide by the laws of the jungle, whereas C & R fishermen think they are above the law.

A key factor in the divide between those who fish for food and those who fish for sport is socio-economic status. Those who can afford it will fish merely as a leisure activity, seeking things like solitude, beauty, challenge, or skill. Almost all fly fishermen fit this category partly because the equipment is expensive but also because fly fishing is not the most effective way of catching fish. If you want trout for food, use corn, worms, or salmon eggs on treble hooks. If you want a challenge and an esoteric set of skills, learn to fly fish.

So this section of the Middle Prong was definitely isolated, in the middle of what is sometimes called the "Middle Prong Wilderness," and probably underfished. Perfect. I had walked over an hour to get to this spot, and it was looking like I might be rewarded for the effort. Of course, I'd never say that out loud because the Fishing Fates would take immediate steps to punish me for my impudence. The basic rule of fishing that we all learn pretty quickly is that no fisherman ever, ever *deserves* to catch fish. You may drive three hours, hike several more, endure Stinging Nettle or briers, and break a few bones – but even after all of that, you should never be so bold as to presume that you've somehow suffered enough to actually deserve to catch a few fish. A day like that will simply confirm what you already suspected – life isn't fair, things don't always balance out, and if things are bad now, they may get better, but they might just get worse. The fact that there seem to be Fishing Fates who lurk around rivers waiting to punish the humble as well as the proud means that fishing is often even less fair than life in general.

I fished in my usual way, which means I tied on a dry fly. Today my fly of choice was a Royal Coachman, a gaudy, old pattern that looks like a tiny Christmas ornament. If you've ever read anything about this fly you've probably seen that "Christmas ornament" description before, but I can assure you that I'm not plagiarizing someone else's original description here. I'm merely giving the most accurate, obvious description available. A Royal Coachman is red, green, and white. The body is a piece of shiny, green peacock feather that looks like tinsel with a segment of bright red thread wrapped around the abdomen. The wing was originally made of feather tips but in recent years is often white calf hair. It's the kind of fly that would be a good practical joke to play on a novice fly fisher – like snipe hunting or secretly putting rocks in a fellow hiker's backpack. The only flaw in that plan is that the Royal Coachman actually works, and no one knows why, which makes me think its origin really was a practical joke that turned sour. I can envision some crusty, old fly fisherman tying up the most ridiculous, dandy fly imaginable and giving it to a novice that he'd be fishing with the next day. He'd justify this cruelty as simply part of male culture – giving the new guy a hard time, establishing the pecking order, and not coincidentally, ensuring that he'd outfish the new guy. You can see how this story has to end. The apprentice outfishes the old master, who promptly goes back to his tying vise and ties up a dozen of his new creation. A new fly is born.

I have absolutely no historical basis for this speculation other than the fact that I can't imagine someone intentionally tying a green, red, and white dry fly. There's simply no logical reason to do such a thing. Dry flies have a long history of being imitations of real, live insects. That's part of the alleged superiority of dry flies. They don't entice a fish to strike out of curiosity or anger or whatever other human passion we want to impose upon them. No. Dry flies, to be fully righteous, are supposed to be reasonable imitations of actual bugs which *fool* the fish into thinking that he's eating a real bug. And there's no such thing as a red, green, and white insect called a Royal Coachman.

I've heard fishing a Royal Coachman compared to going to a bar dressed in a clown suit and trying to pick up women. That's a good analogy for driving home the utter foolishness of fishing this fly... except for one important detail... the Royal Coachman really works. Not all the time. It's not a miracle fly, but it does catch fish. In fact, it caught a few fish for me on this particular day on the Middle Prong, all 6 to 8 inch brook trout. (Yes, the fish are small, but the scenery is really, really pretty....)

If fishing a Royal Coachman isn't brazen enough, I tried something else equally foolish. Let's say the guy goes into the bar dressed in his clown suit and proceeds to openly, proudly pick his nose, and still manages to attract a few women. After catching a few fish in the normal, acceptable way, I switched to the fly fishing equivalent of a clown in a bar picking his nose. I'd let my Royal Coachman float downstream, then at the end of its float, I'd let my fly skitter and dance and drag on the surface, downstream on a tight line. It's a tactic that every experienced fly fisherman has discovered accidentally, found that it can sometimes catch fish when nothing else will, and has sheepishly added it to his arsenal of tactics. And again, today on the Middle Prong, it worked a couple of times. It's the kind of tactic you can use as a last resort when nothing else is working, or when everything else is working just fine and you're just curious.

To most fly fishermen this tactic is near the bottom of the list of acceptability, far below nymph fishing and just a half step above stink bait. Among my circle of fly fishing friends, most simply refuse to fish this way and give me a ruthless taunting when they catch me doing it. Fortunately, none of them were with me today, so I was free to engage in a little harmless deviance with no verbal repercussions. It's a tactic best reserved for times when no one's looking.

Like the clown outfit and nose-picking, using this downstream, tight line tactic just doesn't make sense, and yet it sometimes catches fish, and I don't know why. Some claim it imitates an egg-laying caddisfly or mayfly or stonefly bouncing on the surface, dropping eggs into the water. But all you have to do is watch an egg-laying insect to see that this downstream, tight line tactic bears only a faint resemblance to it, much the way a beaver resembles a buffalo or a hovering osprey resembles a duck on a pond.

Others have suggested that the dancing, dragging fly excites the fish or flips some genetic switch deep in their brain that causes them to chase this object that seems to be fleeing from them. It's the same logic that tells hikers not to turn and run away from a black bear because its instinct will tell it to chase you. Personally, I like this explanation, not because it explains the behavior of trout, but because it explains the behavior of bears. If you are confronted by a black bear in the Smokies, shout and bluff and back slowly away. Throw a couple of rocks. Don't turn and run because, yes, it will probably chase you – maybe to eat you, maybe just to play with you. Either way, you'll end up getting mauled.

What does this have to do with catching trout? Maybe nothing, but it's a theory that explains the trout's tendency to chase my dragging, dancing fly. I'm not saying that this explanation is true. I'm just saying that it works, much like the old Ptolemaic astronomical system worked for over a thousand years. The ancient Egyptian astronomer Ptolemy believed that the earth was the center of the universe and that everything revolves around it. Even though this belief system had things totally backwards, it provided accurate predictions about the movements of the sun, stars, and planets. Most theories about why fish act as they do are like Ptolemy's system. Completely wrong, but they explain perfectly what happens. So, yes, as far as I'm concerned, fish will strike a properly drifting Quill Gordon because they think it's a real Quill Gordon, they'll strike a Royal Coachman out of curiosity, and will strike a dragging dry fly out of instinctive aggression, like a bear chasing a panicked, fleeing hiker. As Ptolemy might have said, "That's my story and I'm sticking to it."

After the trout and I had played around with my Royal Coachman for about an hour, the Fishing Fates (who had been surprisingly gracious so far) had one more trick up their sleeve. They kindly produced a modest Light Cahill hatch. These pale yellow/tan mayflies began to appear on the water's surface as if by magic, so I snipped off my tiny Christmas ornament and tied on a Light Cahill. Now I'd be fishing a legitimate mayfly imitation, the way the good Lord intended.

During this hatch the mayfly nymphs swim from the river bottom to the surface, their skin splits open, and the winged adult pops through the tension of the water's surface. They sit on the surface of the water, being swept downstream while they gain enough strength to fly away to the trees and bushes. There they'll sit for a day or two, waiting for their grand finale in which they'll swarm above the river, mate, drop their eggs into the water, and die. It's the great circle of life. One generation grows and prospers, only to pass the torch to the next.

Or, that's what is *supposed* to happen, but if you'll think about it, that circle of *life* consists partly (fifty percent, I suppose) of *death*. Out there in the natural world, a generation of animals will thrive only at the expense of someone or something else. They don't catch and release; they catch and eat. This is where the fish and birds break into the Light Cahills' circle, and today on the Middle Prong the birds were the first to notice the circle of life beginning to spin.

A few insect-eating birds – mostly flycatchers and an occasional Blue Jay or swallow – moved in quickly. In fact, it was these fly catching birds that first alerted me to the presence of the mayflies in the air and on the water. I'd find myself watching a mayfly who had escaped the fish's jaws flying away, only to be picked out of mid-air be a fluttering flycatcher or a speeding swallow. The flycatchers are nimble and acrobatic. The swallows are so fast and sleek that it sometimes looks like the bug just disappears in mid-air, right before your eyes. The flycatchers handle their prey like a boxer who floats, dances, weaves, and finally strikes; the swallows are like a drive by shooting. I don't know what the Blue Jay was thinking. I had never seen a Blue Jay catch an insect in mid-air, but one did today. He was clearly clumsy and out of his league – like a clown in a bar – but he got himself some.

Soon after the birds became active, I began hearing or seeing an occasional splash of a trout nabbing a mayfly off the surface. When I'd see a splash out of the corner of my eye, I could usually find the spot by locating the ring of ripples moving downstream. I'd cast there, letting my Light Cahill float repeatedly over the spot until the fish decided to take it. Or, to get a better sense of where the fish was, I could watch that general vicinity as another Light Cahill floated by and was sucked in by the fish. Occasionally, a mayfly would bounce along the surface, trying to fly away on tender, new wings, when a trout would jump out of the water and take it in mid-air.

Death from below and death from above. It was pure carnage. These poor mayflies have no defense against this onslaught. In fact, the only thing that guarantees their species' survival is their massive numbers. Like an army, individuals are expendable; it's the species that must survive. And it does. Those few that escape to the trees are like next year's seed corn, the remnant that will produce the next crop of mayflies for the next crop of trout and birds.

This life and death struggle, taking place on a small stretch of a river in the middle of nowhere, was pretty cool... but also a bit sobering. Every moment of every day, we are surrounded by death on a massive scale. Invisible, relentless slaughter. It's interesting, almost entertaining, to stand right in the middle of that struggle and watch it unfold. This is what happens day in and day out in the natural world, whether or not we are present to witness it. Life springs from death in forests and rivers, in front yards and back yards, on roads and lakeshores. This slaughter is invisible, except for those moments when we open our eyes, look around, and realize that no matter where we are, we are standing in the middle of it.

What sets this mayfly hatch apart from a crow eating a dead possum on the road is that this mayfly hatch is usually invisible because we are rarely present to observe it. The mayflies in that twenty yard stretch of water are probably the descendants of the mayflies that have been growing and hatching there for centuries. If the settlers, lumbermen, and sportsmen had shown a bit more restraint, the brook trout in these pools would be the descendants of the brook trout that had been living in this same pool for those same centuries. The circle of life and death turns and turns and turns, usually with no witnesses.

Not long ago, a day like this – easily catching pretty brook trout – would have merely whetted my appetite. Rather than becoming more relaxed as the body count grew, I would have become more anxious, knowing that this wouldn't last forever. I would have fished feverishly until dusk, hoping to catch every last fish that could possibly be caught, but as my days on the river have accumulated, my pace and obsession have diminished. I'm more easily satisfied, which is exactly what happened today. After a couple of hours, sometime during the Light Cahill hatch, I began to focus a bit more on my surroundings and less on the fish. I switched from predator to spectator.

Making that kind of switch is my favorite way to end a day of fishing. It's like finishing a good meal, pushing back from the table, and enjoying the company of family, friends, or a fine cigar while there's still food on the table. This sort of satiated feeling doesn't happen often on the river, but when it does, it's a freeing experience. I've done what I came to do, sooner than I expected, so what's next?

Sometimes I'll just step out of the river and walk away with no regrets, no frustrations. (We talk a lot about the tranquility and beauty of fly fishing. Our dirty little secret is that the most common emotion is frustration.) But today I just sat on a rock in the river, just to get an idea of what the forest and river do while I'm gone.

A Winter Wren sang in the distance, going on and on and on. I can't easily recognize or describe the Winter Wren's song, but I do know that it has the longest song of any mountain bird I know, consisting of a full five seconds of twittering. This little, brown summer resident kept my mind from wandering as I listened intently for his song. The rosebay rhododendron was blooming at this elevation, its wave of white flowers gradually working its way up the mountain slopes as June turned into July. There was the occasional chatter of a red squirrel, the mountain cousin of the gray squirrel of city parks. He's not very red at all, but the hint of orange in his tail is the tell-tale sign that I look for. And he's a little smaller than the gray squirrels that live behind my house. My house... we've been trying to sell it recently. Of course, when your house is on the market, you have to keep the grass green and trimmed.

In spite of the best efforts of the wren, squirrel, and flowers, my mind wandered. I began to drift toward the chores that needed to be done, both at home and at work. The financial obligations. Suffering friends. The price of gas. The front yard. Politics. Responsibility. Irresponsibility.

Is sitting on a rock by a river being irresponsible? Should I hurry home to fix the problems I can fix and worry about those I can't? Or should I stay on this rock, surrounded by the plants and animals of the Smokies, watching their circle turn?

I suppose many people would consider this lazy or irresponsible behavior or maybe just plain boring, wasting time sitting on a rock listening to birds and squirrels. It's funny, isn't it, that a guy who spends a day fishing or walking or sitting in the mountains has some explaining to do, while someone who sits in front of the TV every evening listening to the latest drivel about today's hottest Hollywood celebrity is considered perfectly normal. Why fish or hike or sit when you could be following Paris Hilton's twittering, or better yet, making money? Why sit, doing nothing in the middle of nowhere, so far away from everything?

Barbara Kingsolver, in a story in *Mother Jones* about organic gardening, was asked by her city friends why she lived out in the country "so far away from everything." As she thought about their question, she looked out her window at the yard where her vegetable garden grows, at the pasture where Queen Anne's Lace grows and where deer graze, at the creek at the pasture's edge, at the forest in the distance, and she yearned to ask her frenetic, urban friends: Define "everything."

Thanks, Barbara, for saying it so well. All day long I had not been in the middle of nowhere, far away from everything. On the contrary, to wade and fish in a river, to watch a tiny part of the circle of life and death, to sit on a rock listening to the song of a Winter Wren is to spend a day in the *middle of everything*, which is exactly where I want to be.

Chapter 11
Doxology

"You've gotta see *Easy Rider*, man. It's the greatest movie ever. My life ain't been the same since I saw it... and Jack Nicholson is incredible!"

I didn't know this guy well, just a biker in a biker pub. He was, I'll be generous here, a bit rough around the edges, and I wondered to myself if the change this movie had wrought in his life had been for the better or for the worse. Nevertheless, his enthusiasm was contagious, and besides, *Easy Rider* is one of those classics that everyone is supposed to see. So a couple of weeks later, I watched it, and I'm glad I did because it's kind of cool to be able to say you've seen the *worst* movie ever made. The movie was so bad that when the old guy in the pickup truck pulled up next to Peter Fonda and Dennis Hopper and shot them, my first thought was, "Good! Maybe this movie is almost over. And if not, will someone please shoot *me*?"

Well, that's just my opinion. You may disagree. And that's my point – it's my opinion, no more and no less. When a guy in a bar or on TV tells you how great a movie is, or when I tell you how bad it is, you aren't really learning anything about the movie. You are learning something about the guy who's giving you his opinion. The fact that I hated *Easy Rider* doesn't tell you whether it's a great movie or not. It simply tells you that I didn't like it.

I could tell you how great the Smoky Mountains are, that they are the most dramatic national park in the US, that they provide an unparalleled wilderness adventure, blah, blah, blah. That sort of hyperbole shows up in almost every book or article about every national park in the nation. Pick any national park, at random, and then look at some publications or websites about it, and you'll find someone who thinks that park is the best.

So, is the Great Smoky Mountains National Park the best of all our national parks? To tell you the truth, I don't know and I don't care.

I do know that over 9 million people visit the Smokies every year – more than any other national park – but that number is deceptive. I suspect that many of those people spent more time in Pigeon Forge and Gatlinburg than they did in the park. In fact, their main reason for coming might have been the outlet malls and rides. They may have slipped into the park simply as an afterthought. And I'm sure that being near several major interstates (I-75, I-81, and I-40) that lead from the large population centers of the northeast to the beaches of Florida adds several million visitors to the total.

The Smokies are clearly among the *worst* in some respects. One environmental group ranked the Smokies as the worst major national park for the surrounding towns, congestion, and crowds. I've also seen articles reporting on the pollution problems in the park, especially acid rain. Even some of the park's own literature reports that the views have deteriorated over the past few decades due to smog and air pollution. The Smokies are still *Shaconage* – the land of blue smoke – but now it's due more to pollution than to unadulterated humidity.

But in spite of the problems of pollution and crowds, the Smoky Mountains are a great, great place. They really do provide exceptional opportunities for quiet reflection or exhausting physical activity, whichever end of the spectrum you prefer. As you may have already noticed, I love the Smokies, and I brag on them whenever I get the chance.

But there are others who can praise them more eloquently than I can, such as John Muir, that eloquent eccentric from California. Although he wrote the following words with Yellowstone National Park in mind, they fit the Smokies as well: "Climb the mountains and get their good tidings. Nature's peace will flow into you as sunshine flows into trees. The winds will blow their own freshness into you, and the storms their energy, while cares will drop off like autumn leaves." I believe Muir's message of good tidings, peace, freshness, and energy. A good day in the mountains can resurrect a dying spirit.

But not all days are pleasant. The Smokies can also be a dark, brooding, fearful place. It's a place where the fittest and strongest survive, and their victims don't. It's a place where Boy Scouts get lost and freeze to death, hikers are struck by lightning, and tourists fall in rivers and drown. Sometimes danger sneaks up quietly in the form of hypothermia during a spring thunderstorm. Sometimes it rides in on a bank of March snow clouds and falling temperatures, or lightning bolts during a summer thunderstorm, or a flash flood roaring down the West Prong, or a landslide on the slopes of Anakeesta Ridge. These events are unexpected, which is exactly what makes them deadly. People are caught by surprise, they panic, make one poor decision, or simply weren't paying attention, or were in the wrong place at the wrong time, then they die.

Sometimes we go in search of a challenge and find danger as well. A visit to popular spots like the Chimneys or Charlies Bunion can be dramatic with their steep, rock faces and big views. You stand, squat, or cower on the top near the edge surrounded by empty space. With only a little discretion and physical coordination, these places are safe, but a brief lapse of judgment or a moment of clumsiness can change the lives of your loved ones forever.

Our natural world is a pleasant place if you are well prepared, wise from experience, and a little lucky. Otherwise, it's dangerous and even deadly. Nature should not only be enjoyed, it should also be respected, even feared. It's good, but it's not safe.

I may be reading too much into this paradox of goodness and danger, but in it I see a glimpse of the Creator of it all. A Creator who is not safe, but He's good.

There's a passage in the Bible – the 13th chapter of the book of Hosea – in which God compares Himself and His vengeance to wild animals.

When I fed them, they were satisfied.
When they were satisfied, they became proud...
Like a bear robbed of her cubs,
I will attack them and rip them open.

> Like a lion I will devour them.
> A wild animal will tear them apart.

A scene in C. S. Lewis' *The Lion, The Witch, and The Wardrobe* depicts two of the characters speaking about Aslan, the great Lion of Narnia who symbolizes Christ. Lucy, a young girl, asks one of the inhabitants of Narnia, a talking beaver, if Aslan the heroic Lion is safe. The beaver replies, "Who said anything about safe? Of course he isn't safe! But he's good." That's a pretty good description of the Lion of Narnia, the Lion of Judah, and Mother Nature. They aren't safe, but they are good, and that's what draws us to them.

Epilogue
Do It Yourself

My first exposure to the Smokies was in 1960 when I was 5 years old, and my mother decided that it was time for us to visit relatives in Ohio. From all accounts, I was a pretty good traveler. I enjoyed watching the houses and farms zip by. I wondered aloud why the moon cruised along with us at night, racing past the trees and houses, keeping pace with our Studebaker, going fast when we went fast, slowing to a halt when we stopped for gas. I even enjoyed Ohio with its farms, maple trees, and Amish communities.

This was my first real road trip, and it was all great, but the highlight, by far, was the night that we parked our car in a small, gravel pull-out next to the Oconaluftee River in Cherokee, North Carolina. We slept in the car that night with the wild, relentless sound of the river filling my head. It took me a long time to fall asleep. The sound of the river mesmerized me. Rivers in Florida are slow and quiet, but this one was rocky and loud. It was magical, not to mention probably illegal. Although, those were simpler times, so maybe there wasn't yet a law against sleeping in your car on the side of the road.

Did I say that was the highlight? Well, it was the highlight of my life *up to that point*. Remarkably, the next highlight of my life came the next morning. How lucky can a kid be to have the two highlights of his 5 years of life happen within 12 hours of each other! That foggy, cool, early morning drive through the Great Smoky Mountains was a step into another, better world. It was love at first sight. I learned new place names that in the years to come would become old, familiar friends: Oconaluftee, Newfound Gap, Clingmans Dome, Mount Le Conte, Chimney Tops, Cades Cove, Gatlinburg.

Today as I write this over 50 years later, my wife tells me that I once said, before we were married, that my one wish in life was to live within an hour of the Smokies. Apparently someone heard and granted my wish. It wasn't wasted.

If you'd like to get to know the Smokies better, I hope this book has given you a few ideas of where, when, and how to do it. In the remaining pages I've provided a few more details to help you on your journey.

Chapter 1: Forney Creek
There are four types of overnight camping options in the park, and all require a permit of some sort: developed campgrounds, horse camps, backcountry shelters, and backcountry campsites. The ten developed campgrounds ("frontcounty" camping) are places that you drive to and camp near your car, such as Elkmont, Smokemont, or Big Creek. Most take reservations, while others are first-come, first-served. Most Smokies maps show these campgrounds. For information visit www.nps.gov/grsm, then to make reservations call (877) 444-6777 or go to www.recreation.gov. Horse camps use the same system and same phone and website.

There are about 15 backcountry shelters (mostly on the AT) and about 90 backcountry campsites in the park. They all require reservations, which must be made (no more than 30 days in advance) at https://smokiespermits.nps.gov. These used to be free, but they now cost $4 per person per might. For help or advice call the Backcountry Office at (865) 436-1297. You can also make last minute reservations at the Backcountry Office at Sugarlands Visitor Center.

You can get to Forney Creek on foot by parking at the end of Lakeview Drive – also known as the Road to Nowhere – which starts near Bryson City and heads west several miles into the park. From the end of the road it's only a three mile walk on the Benton MacKaye Trail to Forney Creek.

To paddle to Forney Creek, you'll need to find the boat ramp. It takes about 30 minutes to drive the winding roads from Bryson City to the boat ramp. There may be several ways to get there, but here's the one I know…

If you go to Bryson City via US 74, take exit 64, then US 19 North for 1.7 miles at which point you will bear left onto Old US 19. You will soon see Buckner Branch Road on your left.

Buckner is actually SR 1311, so turn left onto Buckner and check your odometer. Go 3.1 miles on 1311 (Buckner) at which point 1312 (Round Hill Rd.) bears off to the right. Take 1312 to the right and check your odometer again. Travel 2.8 miles on 1312 to a fork in the road where 1312 bears left and 1313 bears right. Take 1313 (right) until it ends at the boat ramp.

An alternative if you are already in Bryson City: Take US 19 South through town. At Walgreens (formerly Kerr) Drug Store check your odometer. Travel 1.1 miles from Walgreens on US 19 South at which point Old US 19 bears off to the right. Take Old US 19 and you will very quickly see Buckner Branch Rd. (SR 1311) on your right. Check your odometer and turn right onto Buckner. Go 3.1 miles on 1311 (Buckner) at which point 1312 (Round Hill Rd.) bears off to the right. Take 1312 to the right and check your odometer again. Travel 2.8 miles on 1312 to a fork in the road where 1312 bears left and 1313 bears right. Take 1313 (right) until it ends at the boat ramp.

Paddling to Forney will take an hour or two from the boat ramp. During summer weekends the lake will be moderately busy – probably a little less traffic than a typical TVA lake. During the off-season, especially on a weekday, the lake will be wonderfully quiet. The further up Forney's channel you go, the quieter it will get – a genuine, mountain wilderness experience.

Once you arrive at the mouth of Forney Creek, just beach your canoe or kayak and walk the 10 minutes to the campsite. Some paddlers will bring a chain and a lock to secure their craft to a tree. If you decide to take a chain, give some thought on exactly how you will attach the chain to your craft. You can't just wrap it around the hull, and most canoes and kayaks don't have many secure beams to run your chain through. (I actually drilled a one inch hole in the top of my kayak to run the chain through.)

To see a map of the park which includes the trails and campsites, choose the *Download Park Maps* link at www.nps.gov/grsm. The free visitor's map that you get at the visitor centers does not show all of the park's trails and campsites. So get the Trail Map, not the Visitor's Map.

There is one other very helpful book that you might want to buy. It's the Bible for hikers in the park – *Hiking Trails of the*

Smokies published by the Great Smoky Mountains Association and edited by Don DeFoe. It gives details on all the trails, shelters, and backcountry campsites in the park. To buy it in a Smokies visitor center just ask for the "brown hiking trails book." They'll know exactly what you mean. To order it online, go to the website of the Great Smoky Mountains Association at www.SmokiesInformation.org.

Even on day hikes, it's a good idea to bring plenty of water and/or a water purification pump. There's no "clean" water anywhere in the backcountry. You have to purify all the water you drink.

A note about getting to Fontana. Of course, it depends on where you are coming from, but if possible you should probably avoid The Dragon. If you ride a motorcycle, you're probably aware of this road. It's Highway 129 along the far SW edge of the park. It's a famous motorcycle route, with 318 curves in 11 miles. (See www.DealsGap.com.) It's a cool road, but it can wear you out in a car or truck. On the other hand, if you are on a motorcycle or a small sports car, don't miss it.

Finally, anyone spending much time in the Smokies ought to get a good map. I'd suggest the National Geographic's Trails Illustrated map #229. It's big, detailed, and water-resistant.

Chapter 2: Sixty-Eight Miles
If you want to do any overnight trips on the AT in the Smokies, you'll have to make shelter reservations at https://smokiespermits.nps.gov. (There are only shelters, no campsites, on the AT.) You are required to stay in these shelters. You can't sleep in a tent on the trail somewhere. You can make shelter reservations no more than 30 days in advance from the *start* of your trip, and that's when you should call. Don't wait until 29 or 28 days ahead. That might be too late. The guidebook called *Hiking Trails of the Smokies* published by the Great Smoky Mountains Association and edited by Don DeFoe is a good guide for the AT in the park (www.SmokiesInformation.org). If you hike the AT *outside* of the Smokies, you don't have to make reservations and you can sleep pretty much wherever you want to. AT guidebooks for outside the park (and inside the park) can be purchased from the

Appalachian Trail Conservancy (formerly Conference) at www.AppalachianTrail.org.

A good, quick introduction to the AT in the Smokies is the four mile hike from Newfound Gap to Charlies Bunion. If you want to do more, consider doing half the park, starting at Newfound Gap (or Clingmans Dome) and walking southwest to Fontana Dam or northeast to Davenport Gap. When my daughter was a teenager, she and I hiked the eastern half of the AT in the park. It was a four-day, three-night trip. After dropping a car off at Davenport Gap (via TN 32 from Cosby or Exit 451 off I-40), we drove to Newfound Gap and started walking that afternoon. We walked only 3 miles and spent the night at Icewater Spring shelter. The second day we hiked 13 miles to TriCorner Knob shelter. The third day we hiked 8 miles to Cosby Knob shelter. The fourth day we hiked 8 miles to the car at Davenport Gap. These mileages were very manageable for both of us. It was almost leisurely. Of course, a 3 night, four day hike from Newfound Gap to Fontana would be a little longer and just as good.

Thanks to James Babb's book entitled *Crosscurrents* for the idea of "experiencing the wilderness" rather than merely "having experiences in the wilderness." Even at my ripe, old age, I tend to bounce back and forth between the two. I guess I still have a few ounces of testosterone flowing through my veins (or wherever it is that testosterone resides).

By the way, most of this story took place around 1979. A few things have changed since then. There's no longer a shelter at Birch Springs; now it's a campsite. Now the AT in the park is about 72 miles, not 68.4. This is due partly to a couple of stretches that were re-routed, but also to remeasuring using more accurate (or at least different) methods. Those of you who are attentive to details will have noticed that the X Files, the Unabomber, and Dollywood didn't exist in 1979. All of the events in this story actually happened, but a few (such as the Unabomber) were on other AT trips in later years.

Chapter 3: Ridges and Rivers
Chapter One's section described the most valuable maps and books. If you walked into a Smokies visitor center and asked a

ranger about hiking and camping, she'd give you pretty much the same list that I gave you.

Chapter 3 introduced you to Mount Le Conte and two of its trails: The Boulevard and Alum Cave Trail. The AT and the Boulevard Trail is a good route – start at Newfound Gap, hike three miles on the AT, turn left on The Boulevard, and hike another 5 miles up to Le Conte.

Alum Cave Trail, my favorite trail in the park, starts from the main road, just a few miles north of Newfound Gap. There's a parking lot (two parking lots, actually) at the trailhead, and it fills up quickly. So, if you are visiting during the peak months of June – October, get there early. It's a great, great trail with lots of character and views. If I do a day hike up Le Conte and back down, this is the trail I usually use.

The other three trails up Le Conte are Bullhead, Trillium Gap, and Rainbow Falls. They are all fine trails. The Rainbow Falls and Trillium Gap trails are two-fer's – that is, you pass a good waterfall on each of these trails. A lot of people hike to the waterfall, then turn around.

There is a rock backpacking shelter on top of Le Conte, but like all the shelters in the park, you can't just show up and stay there. You have to make reservations. The Le Conte Lodge is the more-civilized lodge at the top of Le Conte. It's a very, very popular, high-demand lodge. Reservations are hard to get but would be well worth a try. For more information call (865) 429-5704 or go online to www.LeConteLodge.com.

For a fine day hike that is fairly easy, start at Newfound Gap and walk on the AT *past* The Boulevard trail junction to Icewater Spring shelter. This is a good spot to take a lunch break, but then continue on the AT for another mile to Charlies Bunion. It's a high rocky outcrop with great views. It's every bit as good as the very-popular Chimney Tops hike, but without the hundreds of people. For an added bit of solitude, walk about a quarter mile past Charlies Bunion to the path leading left up a side slope. This leads about 100 yards to a great, usually-lonely viewpoint. To the best of my knowledge, it doesn't have an official name. My friends and I call it the Rocky Crag.

If I were going to make just one day hike in the Smokies, it would be either this Charlies Bunion hike, or Alum Cave Trail, or Mount Cammerer. Of these three, the Charlies Bunion hike is the easiest. Mt. Cammerer is the least crowded. Alum Cave is probably the most crowded, with Charlies Bunion a close second. (Actually, an evening hike up to the Chimney Tops is high on my list. If I write another book I'll probably include a story about it. For now, I'll just say that the Chimney Tops parking lot starts emptying out around 4pm. That's the time to start your hike. Bring a flashlight, in case you linger.)

The reference from Harvey Broome is from his personal journal entitled, *Out Under the Skies of the Great Smokies*. The particular reference to the taste of city water is from his 1944 entry.

Chapter 4: Hazel Creek
To spend some time on Hazel Creek or one of its tributaries, you have two choices: land or water. The land route is rather long and would be a backpacking (and camping) trip of at least one night, probably more. Hiking from Fontana Dam would be about 12 miles one way. If you do much backpacking, then you already know if you are capable of that distance in a single day. If you don't know, that probably means you can't. (For what it's worth, I'm in my late 50s and in moderately good shape, and 10 to 15 miles is about all I care to backpack in a single day, if the weather is good.) The walk from Clingmans Dome is longer, about 16 miles and almost all down hill, including some great main crest hiking. But the walk back out of Hazel to Clingmans Dome would be very tough.

What about a day visit to Hazel? Yes, it can be done comfortably, if you go by water. If you can bring a canoe or kayak with you, then you can easily paddle to the mouth of Hazel Creek, stash your canoe in the woods or chain it to a tree, and walk along Hazel Creek for several hours, then paddle back. It's easily done in one day. There are two boat ramps to choose from. You can go to the Fontana Dam marina and park and put-in there. It's about a 5 mile paddle to Hazel. Or, four miles east of the Fontana Marina on Highway 28 there's a turnoff for Cable Cove Campground. Go north on this road for a bit and find the Cable Cove boat ramp. It's right across the lake from the Hazel Creek inlet. This will reduce your paddle to just 3 miles. This is the put-in that I use when I go to Hazel Creek.

One other water option is the ferry. Details change with the seasons, so call them at (828) 498-2211 and ask for the marina. This ferry is basically a family-sized pontoon boat that will take you from the Fontana Marina to Hazel Creek in the morning and pick you up in the afternoon. Total cost will be about $50 or $60 per person, round trip. They also rent a variety of boats: canoes, kayaks, jet skis, bass boats, pontoon boats.

The historical information about Hazel Creek and Horace Kephart, came mostly from *At Home in the Smokies* by Wilma Dykeman and Jim Stokely, *Hazel Creek From Then Til Now* by Duane Oliver, and *Hiking Trails of the Smokies* by Don Defoe. Of course, Horace Kephart's *Our Southern Highlanders* is an interesting, first-person account of his observations of the last frontier in the eastern US. The Great Smoky Mountain Association also sells a book called *History Hikes of the Smokies* (edited by Kent Cave). It gives the historical background to several of the trails in the park, including Hazel Creek.

Concerning Bone Valley and the dead cows... I've heard two different versions of the story. I described the one that says they were being herded up to the high pasture in the spring when they were caught by a late snowstorm. The other version says they were being herded down in the fall when they were caught by an early snowstorm.

Chapter 5: Long Rod, Short Cast

If you simply want to fish in the Smokies, but not necessarily fly fishing, here's all you need to know. You can't use bait. You must use single hooks, not treble. Technically, it's legal to keep any rainbow or brown trout over 7" long, but most people put them back. (Be sure to wet your hand before you handle the fish. It protects their slimy coating.) The regulations on brook trout are liable to change from year to year and river to river. It's best to assume that you must release any brook trout that you catch, but ask a ranger at the visitor center to be certain. A nice detail about fishing in the park is that you can use either a Tennessee or North Carolina license to fish in the entire park, and you don't need a trout stamp. That means that you could buy a cheap, simple one-day license from either state. They don't sell them in the park, so buy your license outside the park in either state. Go to a visitor center and get their brochure on fishing in the park. It will tell you what I've just told you, plus a few other minor details, including the 3 or 4 streams that might be closed to fishing due to the reintroduction of native brook trout.

If you are interested in fly fishing, there are a few fly shops scattered around. The one I am most familiar with is Little River Outfitters in Townsend. They are a top-notch business with guides and equipment. If you've never fly-fished before, I'm tempted to tell you to learn before you try the Smokies; however, you've got to start somewhere, so why not start here? If you do want to learn a little before you come to the Smokies, there are books and DVDs everywhere. Try Bass Pro, L.L. Bean, Cabela's, Orvis, or YouTube.

A good book to buy for fly fishing in the Smokies is *Great Smoky Mountains National Park Angler's Companion* by Ian Rutter. He's a fly-fishing guide in the Smokies and knows what he's talking about.

Chapter 6: Sunrise, Sunset, And Then Some

This 33 mile day was long and hard but fabulous. If you want to try it, be sure to consider how many hours of daylight you'll have and how you'll handle hiking in the dark, either at the front end or back end, or both. Study the map carefully so you'll know where you'll be and when. We were a little lucky in being at two great spots for sunrise and sunset. That wasn't actually our original plan.

Of course, to do this you need to be a walker/hiker/runner. In other words, make sure you are physically up to the task because there are very few trails in the eastern half of the park to let you bail out in an emergency.

Personally, I'd do it in cool, dry weather. That means October or November, but of course, the days are getting shorter then, so take that into account. This would actually be a good trip during prime leaf season (late October, early November), and because of your early start and late finish, you'd avoid the heavy, leaf-watcher traffic. The fact that you'll be far from any roads in the middle of the day means that you'll see very few hikers. In other words, you can do this hike on even the busiest day of the year, and you'll be fine.

You could possibly do this with no night hiking if you go on one of those long days of summer, but the heat may slow you down so you'll still end up walking some in the dark. Before you decide, try a night hike before you do this trip. See if you like it. Try different phases of the moon as I described in the chapter entitled "Out Under the Moon of the Great Smokies." Bring a flashlight in case of clouds and shade from trees.

One problem will be arranging a shuttle to get back to your car. Since you probably shouldn't do this hike alone, two hikers with two cars may be your best option. A Smokies social networking site that may be helpful in getting advice, rides, or help is http://gosmokies.knoxnews.com.

The writer who wrote about "the consumption of fun and the fun of consumption" is George Ritzer in *The McDonaldization of Society*.

Chapter 7: Out Under The Moon of the Great Smokies
I'm a big fan of Andrews Bald. It's one of only two remaining balds in the park. It's a quick and easy hike. The views are excellent. I can think of no other trail in the Smokies that gives as much bang for the buck as this trail. Whenever someone asks me for a good starter hike in the Smokies, this is the one I suggest.

This is an especially wonderful hike in late June as the flame azaleas are blooming. (The picture on the cover is the trail and flame azaleas on Andrews Bald in late June.) There's a tradition among some Smokies hikers of making a night-time hike up Gregory Bald in late June for the azaleas, preferably under a full moon. I'm not aware of any significant group that does the same for Andrews; although, I'm sure some folks do.

To get to Andrews Bald, park in the Clingmans Dome parking lot and go to the very start of the paved trail to Clingmans. Immediately before the start of this trail, you'll see a small wooden sign and a trail bearing to the left. This is Forney Ridge Trail. Andrews Bald is 1.8 miles down this trail. There's only one sharp, tricky turn on this trail, about 5 minutes into this hike. Take note of it so you don't miss this turn on your way back out. Your walk to Andrews should take about an hour.

I don't do a lot of night hiking, but I'll gladly do it occasionally just to be different or to avoid the crowds. Some people prefer a full moon for their night hiking, and this makes sense as long as you don't need a lot of light immediately after sunset and immediately before sunrise. During these two times, a full moon will be bright but will be low in the sky. That's why I'll usually shoot for a half or three-quarter moon. These will be high in the sky immediately at sunset or sunrise.

Don't wait until you are on your night hike to make sense of these moon phases. Get some practice by going outside of you house before you go to bed. Know what phase the moon is in (waxing or waning) and notice where the moon is at sunset and/or sunrise. You'll learn a lot by spending a few nights observing what the moon is doing.

The terminology I used in describing the moon's phases is common sense terminology, not scientific terminology. What I call the "first half moon" is called the "first quarter moon" by astronomers because the moon is one fourth through its four week cycle. One week later comes the full moon. Then what I call the "second half moon" is called the "last quarter moon" because this second half moon is three fourth through its four week cycle.

The name of this chapter is a play on Harvey Broome's book title: *Out Under the Skies of the Great Smokies*.

Chapter 8: Happy New Year
The story in this chapter took place on the Little River along the road between Townsend and Elkmont Campground. If you want to fish this river, just park at one of the many pullouts and hop in. If you want a bit more privacy, drive to Elkmont Campground and find the sign pointing to the Little River Trail. Park at this trailhead and walk as far as you want. The trail sticks closely to the river for 5 or 6 miles. By the way, this river is called Little River, but it's one of the biggest in the park. Go figure.

You'll be in for a little surprise when you park at the Little River Trail in Elkmont. There are old cottages in varying states of decay scattered around there – the remnants of an old resort that only recent has been finally deserted. Several families had worked out arrangements with the NPS to maintain their rights to this property well into the 1990s. (Present plans are to preserve several of these old buildings.) There's even an old hotel – the Wonderland Hotel – that closed in the mid 1990s and is gradually deteriorating. Now the only lodging in the park is the lodge on Mt. Le Conte.

Also, don't get the Little River confused with the Little Pigeon River, which flows out of the NE quadrant of the park – the Middle Prong of the Little Pigeon is in the Greenbrier area; the West Prong of the Little Pigeon flows along Newfound Gap Road from the main crest, by Sugarlands Visitor Center and out through Gatlinburg and Pigeon Forge. The Little River, on the other hand, starts above Elkmont Campground and flows west toward Townsend.

Although I've written about the Little River here, I'm not claiming that it's the best fishing river in the park. In fact, I'm not sure there is a "best" river for fishing. Some folks would give the title to Hazel Creek, others give it to Abrams Creek flowing out of Cades Cove toward Abrams Falls, and still others to the Little River. It also depends on what you mean by "best." Some folks are willing to sacrifice size and number of fish for the peace and quiet of a secluded river. I can honestly say that you can fish pretty much any main river in the park, and you'll be just fine. They all are pretty decent. Sure there are some dead spots in some of the river, places that are too shallow or too sunny or too warm. The only water I can say for sure to avoid is the stretch of Abrams Creek between Abrams Falls and Abrams Creek Campground at the western edge of the park. As you near the campground, the trout disappear – maybe due to water temperature, or lack of dissolved oxygen, or both, or neither.

My general rule of thumb is that any water that you have to walk a mile or two to get to is ideal. It's just difficult enough that most people won't do it. I'm always looking for opportunities to get a little exercise, so walking 30 or 45 minutes to a good fishing spot kills two birds with one stone.

By the way, if you are wondering what the "small discrepancy" in the calculation of leap year was, here's the explanation. Julius Caesar almost got it right, but not quite. Caesar decreed that every fourth year was a leap year, with February gaining a 29th day. This would work perfectly if every year was exactly 365¼ days long. In other words, in the time it takes the earth to make one trip around the sun, it would spin 365¼ times. However, that last ¼ of a spin doesn't quite happen. The earth finishes its trip around the sun about 11 minutes before the earth spins that last quarter of a turn. The result is that Julius Caesar's leap year adds a full day every four years, which is little too much. Pope Gregory's guys figured out that our calendar has to be tweaked occasionally, which we do every hundred years by *not* adding the 29th day to February – unless the year is evenly divisible by 400, then we *do* add the day. So the year 2000 was a leap year because it was evenly divisible by 400; 2100 won't be a leap year.

Chapter 9: Tsali's Revenge
When you visit Cherokee, if you are interested in the shops and attractions, then you don't need much direction from me. Just drive down the two or three main roads in Cherokee with your eyes open. The attractions are all there and very, very visible. To see the authentic side of things, you should probably start with the Museum of the Cherokee. It's right in the middle of town, next to the Fairgrounds. (They call them the Ceremonial Grounds, although there's not much ceremony that goes on there – it's usually biker rallies and concerts. Once again, jobs and money trump tradition.) Cherokee's website is www.Cherokee-nc.com. I'd suggest that you check this website to make sure there's not a big bike week or some other big event planned at the same time that you'll be there. You might want to see it or you might want to avoid it. Either way, you'll know what to expect.

On the Cherokee website you can find out about the outdoor drama, Unto These Hills, and the recreated Cherokee village, Oconaluftee Indian Village. Yes, it has information on the casino, too.

You might find it interesting to get off the main roads and just drive around the reservation. It's perfectly safe and acceptable. You'll quickly see that the Qualla Reservation looks a lot like any other western North Carolina community. There's very little of the deep, grinding poverty that you'll see at some of the western reservations of South Dakota or Arizona. Tourism has been good, at least financially, to the Cherokee.

You can read the map to see how to get to Cherokee, but there is one detail that's easy to overlook. The Blue Ridge Parkway, a beautiful drive that you shouldn't miss, enters the national park just north of the town of Cherokee. So, if you are arriving from the east, you might avoid some Cherokee traffic by coming in on the Parkway. Or, if you want to bypass Cherokee to get to the park, just come in on the Parkway and head north into the park. The NPS charges several dollars at a toll booth on the Parkway near the entrance, so be prepared to pay.

Notice on your map that Big Cove road leads northeast deeper into the reservation and then Straight Fork road leads into the park from Big Cove. You might want to take some or all of this long, side road. This is a good way to get away from the crowds and into a fairly remote part of the park. One detail is that the Straight Fork Road runs into Balsam Mountain Road, which leads back to the Blue Ridge Parkway. It's a big, long loop that is worth trying, but if you do, you'll have to start on the Parkway and drive this loop north and then back down toward Cherokee. You have to go that direction because the Balsam Mountain road is a one way road. Also, note that this loop is one of those side roads that will be closed from about December to March.

While you are in the Cherokee area, this might be the time to drive west to Bryson City and on to Fontana. In Bryson City the main attractions are tubing down Deep Creek in the summer and the Smoky Mountain Railroad, giving a scenic train ride along the southern edge of the park. Both of these activities are fine. Kids will love them. Give 'em a try.

Just past Bryson City you can take US 74 south to Wesser, NC. The Nantahala Outdoor Center is there, with a lot of whitewater rafting and kayaking opportunities. It's a popular, first-rate operation. Visit www.noc.com.

Also, you can take Hwy 28 west, then at the line between Graham and Swain counties, look for the sign for Tsali Recreation Area in the Nantahala National Forest. (You are in the general area where Tsali's story took place.) There's a boat ramp here and also a good set of trails for hiking, mountain biking, and horse riding. Use of the trails alternates between hikers, horses, and bikes so check their website for the schedule. Try www.fs.usda.gov (then use the Nantahala link) or www.tsalitrails.com or try www.visitnc.com. Or, try an cycling website such as www.mtbikewnc.com.

Of course, Fontana Dam and Lake are in this area. The dam is pretty impressive, so I'd recommend a visit. If you are on a motorcycle, definitely drive west past Fontana Dam and get on US 129 into Tennessee. Those first 10 or 12 miles in Tennessee are the famous Dragon that you've probably heard about. The Dragon is tiring if you are in anything other than a small, low sports car or a motorcycle. If you do make it through the Dragon, staying on US 129 for a few miles is a nice drive along several nice lakes. Or, turn north and drive on the Foothills Parkway that skirts the northwest side of the park.

There were several books and websites that provided a few details for this chapter. Probably the most substantial was www.SmokyMountainNews.com which held several articles by western North Carolina historian George Ellison. I relied on him and *Strangers in High Places* by Michael Frome for the story of Tsali. The original version of the Tsali story by James Mooney is in the *Nineteenth Annual Report of the Bureau of American Ethnology* (1900), partially reprinted by Aldine Publishing in 1975 as *Historical Sketch of the Cherokee*.

Chapter 10: A Day in the Middle of Everything
This would be a good place for me to lie about the location of this day of fishing. (Did I mention that the fish are usually small and the Stinging Nettle is abundant?) I really can't spell out the details of where this fishing spot is because it's one of my favorites simply because it's not fished much. However, if you read this chapter with a map in your hand, you can figure it out.

I usually do these isolated fishing trips in the heat of the summer so I can wet wade and won't have to worry about carrying or wearing waders for several miles. I wouldn't wet wade in March or April, probably not May.

My speculation about the origin of the Royal Coachman is just speculation, based on what I've observed about human nature, male culture, and fishermen. Fly fishing lore places the creation of this fly in 1878 in New York by John Haily and L.C. Orvis.

The "Long Rod, Short Cast" section of this Epilogue has the pertinent information about fishing in the Smokies.

Chapter 11: Doxology
The Smokies are probably less dangerous than some parks. After all, the bears in the Smokies are black bears, not grizzlies. My friend, Greg Harrell, once visited the Gates of the Arctic National Park. He made an interesting observation: at that time most national parks prohibited firearms in the park, but at Gates of the Arctic firearms were *required* in the backcountry. So, yes, nature can be a dangerous place, with some places more dangerous than others.

The Smokies have two types of dangerous snakes: copperheads and timber rattlers. Both have cat-eye pupils rather than round pupils. Yes, that is really how I tell venomous from non-venomous snakes. Bears and wild boar can also give you problems. Realistically, injuries are fairly common in the park, the most common reason being traffic accidents. Now you have another reason to avoid the roads and head to the backcountry. Although, the second leading cause of injuries is slippery rocks in rivers, especially at waterfalls. So don't climb to the top of a waterfall. I'm not opposed to taking risks in life, but only if the potential payoff makes the risk worth it. I don't know what the payoff is for climbing to the top of a waterfall, but it's not enough to justify the risk of crawling up a slippery rock wall. That's just dumb.

One potential danger that doesn't happen often, but it can happen, and it's not something you'd normally think of, is a flash flood. A sudden, isolated rainstorm up near the main crest can suddenly create a wall of water than comes racing down a river destroying everything in its path, including people who are sitting on a rock by the river. This can happen without warning because an isolated thunderstorm can happen several miles upstream near the main crest while the weather is sunny and warm downstream. I've never witnessed it happen, and flash floods really are extremely rare, but when I'm wading in a river I do pay attention to the sky and weather far upstream.

Some reading suggestions from this last chapter... there are several books in the visitor centers (and at the Great Smoky Mountains Association website) about search and rescue missions in national parks that make interesting reading. One popular book about the Smokies is *Lost! A Ranger's Journal of Search and Rescue* by Dwight McCarter.

The John Muir quote in the Doxology chapter is from his book *Our National Parks* (1901). The text of this book is available at www.sierraclub.org.

If you have young kids, C. S. Lewis' *The Lion, The Witch, and the Wardrobe* is a good story to read to them. (The movie is good, too.) I know several people (my wife and I included) who first read this story in their 20s or 30s. It's a story that transcends age categories.

Final Words:

I write an occasional Smokies column called "Rivers and Ridges" in our small, local newspaper, the Jefferson County (Tennessee) *Standard Banner*. I post all my articles (plus a little extra information) on my blog: www.greghoover.blogspot.com. Some of these articles are found in one form or another in this book, but there are also stories in those articles that don't appear in this book, and vice versa. If you'd like to contact me, find me at the social networking site called GoSmokies (http://gosmokies.knoxnews.com). I'm on this site as Greg Hoover. Not a very clever name, but the best I could come up with.

Finally, thanks to Dale Gentry of the *Standard Banner* for giving me the chance to write for his paper and for giving me permission to include some of that material in this book. Also, thanks to my hiking and fishing partners – Greg Harrell, Tim Landefeld, Keith Oakes, and Charlie Roth – for the great times we've shared together and for unwittingly providing the material for these stories. Finally, thanks to my dear, patient wife, Phyllis, for putting up with me for so long.

About the Author

Greg Hoover has lived in Jefferson City, Tennessee since 1987. He teaches Sociology at Carson-Newman University. He received his BA from Atlanta Christian College and PhD from the University of Georgia. He is happily married. He and his wife, Phyllis, have two grown kids, Melissa and Seth, one son-in-law, John, and two grand-daughters, Megan and Julia, who call him "Grampy."

www.ingramcontent.com/pod-product-compliance
Lightning Source LLC
Chambersburg PA
CBHW030439290526
45786CB00001B/357